Challenging Common Myths of Teaching

What are some of the most common myths about teaching and learning? Renowned educator Thomas R. Rosebrough debunks ten popular beliefs and offers principles that will have a bigger impact in the classroom. The principles center on teaching for learners, not only to meet their academic needs but also to transform their lives.

The ten myths explore essential elements of instruction such as curiosity, the place for lecture, engaged learning, how we learn, the role of testing, the importance of challenge and hope and joy in learning, the power of relationships, a focus on teachers' identity as it impacts learning, a new look at the concept of readiness, and the critical development of strategic learning qualities. Key features include the table of Ten Myths and Facts of Pedagogy, the Transformational Pedagogy Model, and the Continuum of Teaching Strategies. Each of the ten chapters includes a device called "Perspective" which provides further insight, practicality, inspiration, and clarity to assist understanding, and "Final Thoughts" which synthesizes and briefly summarizes each chapter.

Whether you're a new teacher seeking best practices, an experienced teacher refining your instruction, or a preservice teacher thinking about what you want your classroom to look like, this book will give you practical solutions, examples, and insights. Read this book in order or jump to your favorite sections. You'll come away with fresh ideas for creating more impactful and joyful learning experiences for your students, so they can see their own potential as critical thinkers and compassionate people.

Thomas R. Rosebrough is the former Executive Dean of the College of Education and Human Studies at Union University. He currently serves as Emeritus Professor of Education, teaching graduate students in educational leadership. Rosebrough has taught at all levels, from elementary school through college, from undergraduate to doctoral education. Rosebrough is the lead author of *Transformational Teaching in the Information Age: Making Why and How We Teach Relevant to Students* (2011). He has published articles in state and national journals including *The Teaching Professor*, articles in two Canadian web journals, book chapters, and frequent columns in various newsletters and newspapers.

Also Available from Routledge Eye on Education

(www.routledge.com/k-12)

Building Executive Function, Second Edition: The Missing Link to Student Achievement
Nancy Sulla

What Great Teachers Do Differently, Third Edition: Nineteen Things That Matter Most
Todd Whitaker

Where Is the Teacher: The Twelve Shifts for Student-Centered Environments
Kyle Wagner

Rigor is NOT a Four-Letter Word, Fourth Edition: Strategies for Success
Barbara R. Blackburn with Melissa Miles

Find Your Blindspot in the Classroom: Improving Your Effectiveness as a Teacher
Anne Bonnycastle

A Lasting Impact in the Classroom and Beyond: Knowledge and Insight for Brave Teachers
Larry Strauss

Transforming Teaching Through Relationship-Building and Self-Reflection: Finding Our Way In
Katherine M. Heavers and Valerie Kearns

Challenging Common Myths of Teaching

Practical Strategies to Transform Learners

Thomas R. Rosebrough

Routledge
Taylor & Francis Group
NEW YORK AND LONDON

First published 2026
by Routledge
605 Third Avenue, New York, NY 10158

and by Routledge
4 Park Square, Milton Park, Abingdon, Oxon, OX14 4RN

Routledge is an imprint of the Taylor & Francis Group, an informa business

© 2026 Thomas R. Rosebrough

The right of Thomas R. Rosebrough to be identified as author of this work has been asserted in accordance with sections 77 and 78 of the Copyright, Designs and Patents Act 1988.

All rights reserved. No part of this book may be reprinted or reproduced or utilised in any form or by any electronic, mechanical, or other means, now known or hereafter invented, including photocopying and recording, or in any information storage or retrieval system, without permission in writing from the publishers.

Trademark notice: Product or corporate names may be trademarks or registered trademarks and are used only for identification and explanation without intent to infringe.

ISBN: 978-1-041-08809-7 (hbk)
ISBN: 978-1-041-08805-9 (pbk)
ISBN: 978-1-003-64704-1 (ebk)

DOI: 10.4324/9781003647041

Typeset in Palatino
by codeMantra

To Bonnie

Contents

Meet the Author viii
Prologue x

    Introduction 1

1 Nurturing Curiosity 14

2 Embracing Lecture 25

3 Engaging Learners 37

4 Discovering How We Learn 55

5 Testing, Testing 70

6 Challenging Learners and Building Hope 85

7 Finding Joy in Learning 97

8 Prioritizing Relationships 109

9 Securing Teacher Identity 128

10 Fostering Student-Centered Teaching 145

    Conclusion 162

    References 182

Meet the Author

Tom Rosebrough represents a wealth of teaching and leadership experience. His interest in teaching has lasted a lifetime because he has always considered students and their holistic potential as the priority of education. He has taught public school and students at all levels (reading, mathematics, and social studies) and university students both private and public, undergraduate and graduate. Tom is from Ohio where he graduated from public schools, attended Ohio University, Miami University (where he student-taught at the William McGuffey Laboratory School), and then Ohio State University with a degree in History. Perhaps the last five letters of the word "history" inspired a career dedicated to the individual stories of children. He earned the MA and PhD from Ohio State in Early and Middle Childhood Education, and did postdoctoral work at Harvard University. As a leader he served as program director, chair, dean, and executive dean at three Christian liberal arts universities. He considers academic leadership as an outgrowth and extension of scholarly pedagogy. His signature work and research on the transformational teaching framework has been widely recognized. Under his administrative watch at Union University, undergraduate and graduate programs were nationally accredited and honored as a Model of Excellence in holistic teaching, growing in enrollment into one of the largest at the university, resulting in a center for educational practice bearing his honorary namesake. *Challenging Common Myths of Teaching: Practical Strategies to Transform Learners*

is the latest of his scholarly endeavors in books, articles, and national and international presentations. To his delight, colleagues planted a Buckeye Tree on campus to honor his retirement as a long-serving Executive Dean, and he now serves as Emeritus Professor of Education. Tom and his wife have two children and two grandchildren, and currently reside in Tennessee.

Prologue

Life is often about balance. Poet Samuel Taylor Coleridge said that imagination is revealed "in the balance or reconciliation of opposite qualities." While our curiosity leads us toward learning and often a wide range of emotions, our passions and enthusiasms can lead us toward more immoderate experiences and we learn from our mistakes if we are wise. Individually we can learn to balance humility with self-confidence. Likewise, the world of education is full of opportunities and interactions which can teach us balance for the sake of our young students. Hopefully our moral compasses will lead us toward what historian Jon Meacham calls the "sensible center."

Extremes in education seem to occur often with standardization being the most recent malady. Our current U.S. schools came from extremity. Only a brief study of the modern age of education reveals both the depth of what we have learned about pedagogy and the extremes we enlist. We could place a historical marker on educational modernity with John Amos Comenius in the 17th century (in modern-day Czech Republic) and his fight for the psychological individuality of children (he said children are not miniature adults), or with Martin Luther (Germany) in the 16th century as he championed universal elementary education (boys and girls, all social classes). Both men sensed the need for a more holistic educational philosophy in their turbulent times.

Standardization of schooling has occurred despite major findings in research and best practice that should point the United States in a different direction in this century. Over the past 60–70 years the quest in educational research (Richardson, 2008) has shifted from solely promoting intellectual development to how teachers can actively engage learners in more holistic ways. Even intelligence is newly defined not by "how smart we are," but "how we are smart."

Methods have included integrating multimedia into lectures, using learner voting systems to speed communication with teachers, employing the internet to encourage collaboration, and providing preinstruction lecture notes and videos (Slavich & Zimbardo, 2012). Higher education, where the pedagogy of lecture (Twenge, 2009) still dominates, has been impacted, but many teachers at all levels are reconsidering what matters and how to accomplish what is needed.

At the turn of the 21st century the old dichotomy between traditional (subject-centered) and progressive (student-centered) philosophies of education still held sway, but an amalgam of more student-centered and active learning pedagogies began to take hold at least in the world of educational psychology and philosophy, and somewhat in practice. The effect has been a moderating shift in how educators view teaching and learning. The term "transformational leadership" has been a salient part of the culture in business, politics, and education for a long time, at least a half century. But the word "transformational" has only recently been applied to teaching and learning. I think it is time to stamp "transformational teaching" onto our academic conversation in the discipline of Education.

History Speaks to Us

We can gain vital perspective from educational theory. Lev Vygotsky and Jean Piaget were 20th-century theoretical giants who echoed the importance of a richly engaging and supportive classroom environment. Vygotsky's (1978) social constructivism involves beliefs and understandings shaped by learners' historical, social, and cultural contexts. Where students live and learn matters. Their self-identity and efficacy matter. Who their teacher is, really matters.

Vygotsky expanded Piaget's (1926) constructivist notion to include the dynamic of teacher support for closing the gap between performance and development of students. Piaget researched and advocated for more student interaction with objects in the physical world as well as with peers in a problem-solving format in order to produce cognitive dissonance. Such dissonance occurs when new knowledge and experiences seem to conflict with formerly assimilated learning. Piaget encouraged learning activities which required higher-order thinking skills of analysis, synthesis, and evaluation (Svinivki & McKeachie, 2011). New frameworks and methods are needed in this century to maximize both intellectual potential and personal growth (Slavich & Zimbardo, 2012). Transformational teaching and learning is a new comprehensive framework.

Education has nearly always mirrored the perceived needs of society. K-12 U.S. education has gravitated to extremes in curriculum and methodology over the last 100 years. Witness the excesses of progressive schools with unruly students and laisse faire teachers which were misguided applications of John Dewey's ideas in the 1920s, to the Skinnerian behavioral objectives and teaching machines of the 1970s and 1980s. In between were the reactive back-to-basics schools of the 1930s influenced by John B. Watson, and the open, informal education schools of the late 1960s and early 1970s in classrooms without walls. Now we have the standardized teaching-to-the-annual-test era of the first three decades of the 21st century where test scores seemingly substitute for learning.

Why do we behave this way in the education of our youth? We want the best for our children and we fear letting them down with their schooling. Our fears lead us toward risking extremes in schooling. Laypeople are influenced by what "experts" say and do, trusting in their authority to provide good schools and teachers for their children. Mandated standardized assessments stoke fears of failure and now we see others "succeeding" with test meritocracies across the world. Politicians grab for simplistic solutions and throw exorbitant amounts of money at complex problems. Our current curse of standardization is traditional education morphed to an extreme.

Undergirding our fears in education is the tendency to ignore research and best practice. The term "best practice" should connote a well-considered synthesis of what we know from good theory, research, and experience. Instead, our tendency is to bathe in ignorance as we create mythologies about how we should teach and how students learn. Our current era of schooling in the United States has embraced pedagogical fiction and denied facts in a myopic competitive dance with world cultures of schooling. How can we return to a sensible center where the holism of student potential is prized?

Transformational Teaching and Learning

How do students learn? How should teachers teach? What does excellent schooling look like? This book seeks to paint that picture by challenging the myths of teaching in positing theory, research, and best practice. Exposing myths and exploring facts of pedagogy can be thought-provoking for teachers. We educators need guidance on knowing, believing, and doing. This author's way of approaching this guidance is through the power of an idea, a conceptual framework called transformational pedagogy. This text explores *transformational teaching and learning*, where teachers can teach to transform all students learning to their potential. Wordsworth captured some of the joy and wonder of a child's learning via a seashell:

Applying to his ear the convolutions of a smooth-lipped shell,

To which, in silence hushed, his very soul

Listened intensely, and his countenance soon brightened with joy.

Learning is a complex subject, but the term transformational learning communicates well, speaking directly to a significant change in our students. It is a student-centered term inferring that we should teach to transform, not just inform, learners. While teaching and learning are very separate actions (which for some is a point of dispute), they are also meant to be synergistically connected. To achieve synergy in the teacher-student dynamic, the goal of teaching (Rosebrough & Leverett, 2011) must be to transform learners academically, socially, and spiritually. Holism in education means we do not settle for less. A caveat here: No measure of commitment to holistic goals can overcome teachers' weak academic preparation and poor planning. In a phrase, we should want it all for our teachers and learners, because all is required for transformation.

"Spiritual goals" as a part of transforming learners is used with intentionality to explore the concept of personal growth in students. It certainly holds a very personal connotation, even religious for many. We contrasted it with "social goals" for effect. Transformational teachers can lead students toward self-discovery involving basic beliefs about themselves. The journey can transform students' dispositions toward learning by increasing self-efficacy, agency, self-directed learning skills and qualities, and hopeful attitudes. Duckworth's (2016) conception of "grit" places it firmly as a noncognitive, even spiritual trait tied to a person's passion and perseverance with long-term goals. She argues that successful people's real genius is grit, not necessarily intellect.

We also employed the term "teacher-relater" to highlight the process of creating dynamic teacher-student relationships that can incubate transformational learning. Inspirational teachers are needed. Relevant information is needed as well, but inspiration must precede information as a priority.

In 2005, educational psychologist George Slavich introduced *transformational teaching* as a term to describe instruction that promotes meaningful change in students' lives. In 2011, before the repetitive excesses of standardized education fully kicked in and began to impact schools and students in the United States, Ralph Leverett and I, in what seems to have been the first book on the topic, proposed a full-fledged model, the *Transformational Pedagogy Model* (TPM), as a holistic antidote for lockstep, test-prep schools as well as for silo models of subject-centered education.

In this book, the TPM serves as a pedagogical fulcrum for a contemporary analysis of ten myths and facts of teaching. The table of Myth and Facts found in the "Introduction" is the lever for prying open and exploring the concept of *transformational learning*. It takes a transformational teacher to produce transformational learning.

Change within the System

The act of exposing myths and exploring the facts of pedagogy in itself will not change the educational world. It *can* transform schools if, as a result, educators hearken to the contrast and begin to teach and lead at the human level. Fred Rogers' (aka Mister Rogers) favorite saying was from *The Little Prince*: "That which is essential is invisible to the eye." If we allow change in ourselves we can change the world.

Such change is difficult unless we step back and seek context, perhaps taking a 21st-century drone's-eye view of our educational culture with the assistance of historical perspective. We will not change anything in our schools if we continue to succumb to what historian Jon Meacham (2006) terms the "tyranny of the present." He writes,

> To fail to consult the past consigns us to what might be called the tyranny of the present—the mistaken idea that the crises of our own time are unprecedented and that we have to solve them without experience to guide us. Subject to such tyranny, we are more likely to take a narrow or simplistic view, or to let our passions get the better of our reason.

Meacham continues,

> If we know, however, how those who came before us found the ways and means to surmount the difficulties of their age, we stand a far better chance of acting in the moment with perspective and measured judgment. Light can neither enter into nor emanate from a closed mind.
>
> (p. 232)

This book is an attempt to capture and illuminate this moment in the education of our youth with a hopeful perspective and measured judgment. I believe our schooling, perhaps at all levels, can do better by renewing its attention to a foundation of good theory and practice in pedagogy.

Standardized education is a generalized term, but it is apt and inclusive because by its nature it promotes closed minds to the transforming potential of teaching and learning. What a historian writes about U.S. society is certainly applicable to our troubled 21st-century schools. We have failed to consult past and current research and experience in our drive to narrow and simplify a complex concept of *pedagogy*, which is the art and science of teaching and learning.

Allowing change in ourselves promotes change in practice. While change in practice is a desired end, we in the discipline of education must not chronically cling to the "practics of doing" in isolation from theory and research. As a leader in teacher-preparation, I learned that some professors gravitated toward the practics of instruction while others tended to embrace theory. In my role I tried to encourage every professor (and myself) to choose the "divine and," to work hard to represent theory *and* practice. They need and deserve connection.

Theory into Practice

Students are asking us not only, "What can I do?" but also, "Who can I be?" In life we know that a well-chosen word can be like a drink of water to a thirsty soul. Sometimes only water will do, but words and actions can coexist. Teaching is a relational profession where our habits of practice not only depend upon good theory and research, but define our identity as teachers. While not diminishing or belittling the role of good methodology, *knowing* for a teacher can be *doing* for a teacher. Knowing a subject and good theory is a form of practice. Is knowing enough when we meet our students on Monday morning? Sometimes. But theory-only creates pathos with learners, while practice-only fashions a steady descent into random chaos. "Theory into practice" is a good teacher's mantra.

Comenius was a brilliant 17th-century Czech educator, arguably the father of modern education. He was among the first to stand up for children as children in development. He wrote a book called *Orbis Pictus*, meaning *A World with Pictures*. He realized that learners, especially young ones, need pictures to understand words. *Orbis Pictus* was an alphabet book that associated pictures with letters and words. In the classic King James English language: D is for Duck. "The duck quacketh," followed by a cute picture of a duck quacking.

Johann Pestalozzi bridged the 18th and 19th centuries as a Swiss educator, sometimes called the father of pedagogy. Among other innovative ideas he took Comenius' theories a step further with "object lessons." A religious man like Comenius, he believed education is about head, heart, *and* hands. Learners, especially children, need hands-on experiences where they can hold a wooden duck (or even a live one). He was instrumental in inspiring Friedrich Froebel, a German mathematician, to create the practics of a classroom garden for young children, the kindergarten.

Completing this trilogy of classic theorists in education, the 20th century saw educational psychologist Jerome Bruner link the concrete, the pictorial, and the abstract in the teaching of mathematics to young students. Children can best understand the number seven by starting with 7 little plastic ducks, then 7 pictures of ducks, then the numeral 7 which is the abstract symbol for the number seven. It is a mistake to proceed in the opposite order, beginning with the abstract (or symbolic). Knowing theory can be a form of practice for teachers. Research supports the theory while practice confirms it.

The "strawman" in this book is standardization of our schools with its debilitating effects upon teachers and students alike, but the practice of organizing educational efforts with high expectations called standards and holding educators and students accountable is not blame-worthy in itself. Such practice is likely well-intended, but not well-informed when taken to the extremes of educator-accountability and subject-centered pedagogy. For example, two of the iconic bastions of teaching are lecture and testing, not by any stretch bad practices in themselves, but now over-practiced. The problem occurs when we create a system that promotes rigid teaching standard-by-standard, excessive summative testing that holds teachers and schools accountable for factors they cannot control, and students being left by the wayside in our priorities.

The system has to change, but in the "meantime," transformational teachers can still teach to human potential by serving as models of knowing, doing, and relating, as prototypes of best practice. Great teachers have always rowed against the currents.

This writing is meant to compare, search for, and identify the salient "facts" of a balanced pedagogy. Seeking balance can sometimes seem like listening to the ocean in a seashell, but when achieved can lead to the joy of transformational learning.

With Gratitude

My teacher-experience is not uncommon. In a phrase, *by teaching, we learn*. I am grateful for my students over the years who have taught me so much more than I have taught them: K-12 students, undergraduate students, and now especially graduate students in education—experienced teachers and leaders—who have shared their professional lives with me. This book is a small reflection of the depth of my discourse with them, embedding and embracing their stories and wisdom about transformational teaching and learning.

Introduction

William Butler Yeats reportedly said, "Teaching is not the filling of a pail but the lighting of a fire." It is a fact of most of our lives that teachers are seen as pail-fillers. I suspect this is because as a profession, teaching embraces a form of mythology. The overall mythology of teaching is that it is a process of pouring out information based on expectations often called standards, that the best teachers are those who present well, and that there is a necessary relationship between what is "taught" and what is learned by students. This is tri-fiction of course. Learning science research (Blumenfeld et al., 2006; Bruning et al., 2011; Jensen & McConchie, 2020) is very clear how humans learn in individual ways as we build upon past experiences. We can meet students where they are, adapt our methods, monitor progress formatively, teach to change their lives, and we have not taught unless learning has taken place.

    The salient problem is that most educators begin with expectations related to the teacher or to a subject instead of directly to learners. We walk away from a presentation or other classroom experience saying, "I feel good about today. The words came easily for me and I think the students learned," only to find on a subsequent quiz or other assessment that few had learned anything. We spend our time thinking about ourselves in what and how we teach and very little time on how our students learn. Good pedagogy comes from the inside out—inside the student and out to the teacher. Sensitivity to students' learning is the starting point of good teaching.

We live in an age in public schools where standardized thinking rules, which is a direct response to the concern for many years, even before NCLB, that the U.S. education system is falling behind. The concern is well-founded, but the macro-level solutions lack validity. Throwing the wrong solution at a problem makes the problem worse.

Perspective: Getting Real

The real issue of our day is that government blames teachers for low test scores and failing schools, regardless of the complexity of the problem. Postman and Weingartner (1969) compared this kind of simplistic thought to wacky doctors giving penicillin to every sick patient, regardless of their malady. "Why?" someone asked the doctors. The answer: "Bad patients, son, bad patients." If our schools are sick, it's "bad teachers, son, bad teachers." The "solution" has made victims out of teachers and hence, their students. Teachers are blamed and held accountable for things they cannot control. The problem has gotten worse, as national and international data confirm. Simple answers don't fix complex problems, and how humans learn is a complex phenomenon.

The contemporary reality is that we are still regressing because of uninformed policy based on a fallacious input/output psychology of learning. It is behaviorism redux, where policymakers and now school authorities believe most learning is acquired through conditioning, which is a process of reinforcement and punishment. The "heart" of behavioral psychology is worldview-like: Students are like subjects in a study to be manipulated. The outside world acts on them; they are not expected to be actors upon the world. The reason we hear so much talk about student and teacher and leader agency is that students and teachers and leaders have lost control of their own moral and creative agendas. The data is clear on the failure of standardized pedagogy.

Program for International Student Achievement (PISA) 2022 results, published in December 2023, with 85 countries (Barshay, 2023) are dismal for the United States. PISA 2018 results (pre-Covid

19) were just as dismal. Mathematics is particularly low on each of the latest PISAs: Only 7% of U.S. students are able to do mathematics at advanced levels. In reading and science, the United States basically stayed the same over two decades. Asian countries are still dominant in PISA scores, just as they were in 2006.

The NAEP (the "nation's report card") for 2022 reports that 39% of fourth and eighth graders in U.S. public schools are below basic proficiency, 4 points "up" from 35% in 2019. Almost 40% of our children cannot read and compute at even the basic level of achievement some 20 years into the alphabet soup of NCLB (2001), RTTT (2009), and ESSA (2016). Black and Hispanic students scored far below Asian and white students.

National and international studies are highlighting what many educators are living firsthand. Impersonalized and narrowly conceived school policy and pedagogy is failing U.S. education. It takes a transformational culture to raise public schools, and power and money cannot define success. There are beacons of light in public schools with the flexibility of thought to promote differentiation, accept and utilize multiple intelligence theory, encourage growth mindset practices, use test results for individual diagnosis of student learning needs, and facilitate self-directed learning through guided inquiry. Unfortunately these bright lights are the exceptions not the rule. U.S. public schools have been pressured and sometimes mandated to throw away their educational identity of creativity and adventure in order to imitate countries with exam meritocracies.

The measures of lockstep education are political and tragic, making it essential that educators rethink what we are doing. If we are to begin with expectations related to learners, which is the beginning of transformational learning theory and practice, we must start by asking, "What is learning anyway?"

Learning Theory

Educational psychologist Jeanne Ormrod (2012) defines learning as "a long-term change in mental representations or associations as a result of experience" (p. 4). She explains that while learning is a long-term change, it doesn't necessarily last forever. Ergo, we forget things. This reference is meant to be in a cognitive context, as in mental associations in the brain (which behaviorists deny exist because they cannot be readily observed). And, she emphasizes learning as a change from experience as compared to physiological maturation or change from dysfunctional behavior.

Note the words "learning as a change from experience." Learning involves *change* and *experience*. The phrase "*from* experience" should not be overlooked. Our teaching should make something happen that is somehow beyond the existing experience of the learner. This change from experience begins, however, with teachers' connecting to the existing experiences of students. Education is about changing or transforming students by providing experiences in rich learning environments. Education reaches beyond informational teaching and is much more than feeding the intellect.

We teach for learners, not only to meet their academic needs but also to transform their lives. Transformational teachers want more than academic or intellectual change. A certain sensitivity is needed in reaching students through their emotions, which are surprising gateways to brain-compatible learning. And, whether realized or not, students desire the holistic transformation that reaches to their spiritual essence, which is a lasting change because it is who they are.

Perspective: Inspiration Before Information

Manuel always wanted to be a teacher who made a difference. By teaching mathematics in middle school he knew he had opportunities. When he was a student "back in the day," he learned that every one of his teachers approached teaching differently. As he reflected upon his favorite and most impactful teachers, however, he realized he wanted to be more like Mr. Todd, a high school physics teacher. This man always seemed to enjoy what he did. And, he always seemed to have something new; that is, Mr. Todd loved his subject and Manuel never got the impression that his teacher had taught a particular lesson many times before (even though he had). This dynamism affected Mr. Todd's students—they were "with him" even though his class was difficult. He cared. That's what Manuel wanted for his students—to reach his students at a deeply personal level to transform them into steady, if not passionate, life-long learners.

Teaching is attitudinal in its essence. We have to know who learners are and care about how they learn. Lately in our more standardized era we do study what learners are learning but mostly in a summative context and not a diagnostic sense. The overall persisting mythology is that teaching is something we do *to* someone rather than *with* someone.

An iconic line from a classic Western film may help us understand the persistence of misplaced belief in what teaching is. "When the legend becomes fact, print the legend," was the line delivered by a newspaper editor in the movie. When fiction becomes fact, print fiction. The fiction is that the best teachers play the "sage on the stage" role. Frankly, there is enough truth in this idea to convince many that it is accurate. Some of our best teachers are wise and articulate as lecturers/presenters. The fact is, however, that great teaching begins with the learner. If a false or misleading idea is repeated enough, we tend to believe it. We become habitual instead of reflective in thought. Perception becomes reality but the perception along with the ongoing reality is based on fiction.

There is indeed fact and fiction in education. Long has been a misperception related to teacher roles, but contemporary culture in terms of entertainment and media consumption is still dominated by the idea that the role of the teacher is a "jug-to-mug" affair. Simple is better (and more saleable) for policymakers in their tunnel-visioned effort to raise achievement scores, to wit: Set high standards, teach to them, test for them, punish or reward schools and teachers. In many U.S. public schools, educational standards are to be followed like a recipe book, mandating that we should connect subject matter to them and teach to them via pacing guides, and then see what kind of cake we cooked at the end of the year. This is a tragically misguided notion.

Perspective: Using Standards

Standards are guides or signposts or launching pads for teacher creativity and connecting to the individual experiences of learners. Imposed curriculum is a teaching reality; and, indeed the year-end achievement test is ever-present in our school cultures. Let's understand: Tests are good when they inform student learning through accountability—we must know if we

> are succeeding as educators. Standards are vital in defining expectations and guiding learning. Without the structure of standards, for example, schools would struggle to developmentally differentiate the grade levels. But despite the allure and persuasion of "high standards," they are not a panacea for success in education, especially when they are assiduously tied to lockstep teaching and testing.

David Berliner (2011) was an early-on critic of high-stakes testing and its effects on curriculum and learning. He made the case that the most rational but also the most pernicious trait of standardized schools in the United States and Britain is what he termed "curriculum narrowing." When teachers are all but required to teach to the test, a narrowing occurs that reduces many learners' chances of being "thought talented" (Berliner's term) in school. The result is a restriction of creative and purely enjoyable activities. Ultimately, he predicted, the reform policies ensure that many of the skills needed for the 21st century will not be taught. Standardized education is failing.

Perspective: Predicting the Future

While no one should pretend to know exactly what knowledge and skills our students will need for an uncertain future, David Berliner is compelling as he voices words about schooling and what teachers need, and it is not standardized education. He would be justified in quoting Lord Byron:

> *Of all the horrid, hideous notes of woe,*
> *Sadder than owl-songs or the midnight blast,*
> *Is that portentous phrase, "I told you so."*

Some have developed ideas recently that assist beleaguered educators. Carol Dweck (2007, 2017) and her associates have expanded the thinking of teachers with their growth mindset theory. For them good teachers believe that learners can change with practice especially after errors and failure, while misguided educators still cling to a fixed mindset that growth cannot occur because of unchanging abilities. The theory struck a chord among people who saw what standardized education is doing to students. Motivation as a variable is virtually ignored in standardized, information-based models. The growth mindset theory strikes against the idea that high ability lessens the need for effort. Instead, we should praise work ethics, not scores on standardized tests. Learners have both growth and fixed mindsets at different times. Nurturing teachers feed a growth mindset but they also can connect to the fixed natures of individuals.

Dweck's work is a bit of a bridge from the developmental psychology of Piaget and Vygotsky, adding to the both-an argument of nature versus nurture in learning. Eric Jensen (2019) writes of specific high-impact mindsets that are effective in impoverished school settings: relational, achievement, rich classroom climate, engagement, positivity, enrichment, and graduation mindsets. The key is in creating a welcoming and curriculum-rich classroom environment where students love to learn.

Creating rich learning environments begins with teacher attitudes vital to educating students to their potential. Teaching is complex, not simple.

Perspective: Complexity and Dr. Death

How do we know it is complex? One overriding reason is that the myth-makers' "teaching" can and does occur without learning. A second reason lies in the very nature of learners; they are complex human beings with diverse experience, knowledge, and motivation. A third reason can be found in teachers themselves. I once knew a college professor who taught mathematics and called himself "Dr. Death." He was an extreme example of someone who lorded his superior knowledge and did not mind failing students. He had an attitude problem, and fortunately he did not last long in the profession. He would have thought that teaching to the whole learner was somehow mushy and squishy, lacking credence. His subject (and perhaps himself) was at the center of his pedagogy model.

Holism is a mutual dynamic. We are changed as our students change. It takes a whole teacher to teach a whole student. It takes a transformational teacher.

Transformational Teaching

To change the current informational teaching paradigm, to transform thinking and transform lives, we must view our students as full of individual promise. We can teach with a mindset of change if we want to transform the cultures of our schools, and we cannot meet transformation as a goal without supportive and enriching classroom environments. Transformational learning does not necessarily occur in a classroom. It can occur in a classroom "dining in," but it often happens as "take-out" reflection because time is always a factor in learning. Transformation occurs at a deeper level than the academic.

The term "transformational teaching" was used by Slavich (2005) to convey that teachers can promote meaningful change in students' lives, depending on how they perceive learners. In 2011, Ralph Leverett and I presented a comprehensive pedagogy model showing that transformational teaching is teaching designed to change learners academically, socially, and spiritually, and that teachers need a holism of roles to meet the holistic needs of students. Rigor in academics is the floor not the ceiling—we can expect more. We reach for the stars when we teach to full human potential. As teachers, why settle for a technician-like approach with no reverence for the human spirit, no enduring passion for learning?

Why settle for just informational teaching?

Perspective: Don't Settle!

When someone performs a service for us, let's say a mechanic putting in a car battery or maybe an alternator, our first concern is usually their knowledge and skill (and cost!). But, we also are affected by their manner, or friendliness. If they are prosocial in personality and honest in character during the transaction, we are a lot more likely to return to them for service next time. Education is like that. At its best it is multifaceted and motivational. Students need what John Dewey called "educative" experiences which encourage them to continue learning, not miseducation which stifles growth. Why settle for a narrow one-and-done learning experience that represents basic expectations? Transformational learning is about expectational returns that continue for a lifetime.

We equate strong standards with academics alone, an unfortunate equation. High expectations do positively affect human behavior, but teaching needs a philosophic mantra of "wanting it all" tied directly to students' academic, social, and spiritual needs. Patricia Cranton (2002) and more recently ASCD/ISTE (2024) have articulated principles of transformational learning. The effort to prioritize holism and transform the learner is not only desirable but highly appropriate pertaining to educational research. The challenge is to articulate a description of something as complex as learning in simple terms. As Einstein reminded us, if we cannot say it simply, we likely do not know what it is.

The dynamic that is transformation includes the *teacher* and the *curriculum* as well as the *learner*. Pedagogy is the art and science of teaching and learning, an inclusive definition meant to capture a complex synergy among the three entities. We (2011) explained this dynamic with a pedagogy mantra of: *Why we teach = Who we teach*. We developed the "Transformational Pedagogy Model" (TPM) as a contrast to the national onslaught of standardized thinking in public schools, hoping to infuse holistic education into the mix with the goal of transforming learners.

Notice the TPM looks like a target with "The Learner" placed in the center, not subject matter. Encompassing the center is an inside ring for the *transformational teacher* roles of Scholar, Practitioner, and Relater. Scholars have reason to be confident in what they know, not just their subject but also good learning theory and research; practitioners are creatively attuned in how to teach; and, relaters care for their learners in holistic ways. The rather unique term, relater, was chosen to connote the power of relationships as a significant part of a teacher's roles. Finally, the outside ring of the model contains the three goals of Academic, Social, and Spiritual, speaking to the holism of knowledge (Figure 0.1).

To transform lives, schools and classrooms must include relevant knowledge in past, present, and future-oriented curriculum but also teach to the overall well-being of learners socially (respect for others, cooperation, sharing) and spiritually (self-respect, self-efficacy, fostering hope, perseverance).

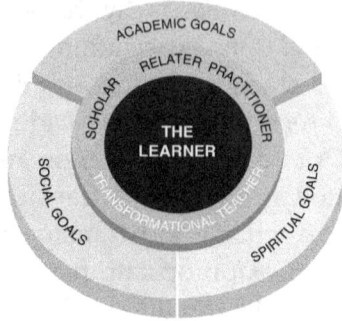

TRANSFORMATIONAL PEDAGOGY MODEL

Figure 0.1 Transformational Pedagogy Model. Copyright 2011 by ASCD.

Elementary school leader, Kris, has summarized: "This is the process known as transformational teaching. It stretches beyond the *how* of instruction; it crosses over the *what* of content; and it settles upon the *who* of learning." Note that she said "process," which is generally defined as a series of actions toward a desired goal. The desired goal is first to connect to and then positively change students' lives. What transformational teaching is not, is a single methodology or philosophy. It is also not some new innovative program, but a synthesis of and framework for what has always worked when we center on students. We likely have enough innovations to choose from already.

Perspective: Row the Boat

Great teaching is and always has been like rowing upstream. It requires us to work harder than the rest. Kahlil Gibran wrote that "work is love made visible." Transformational teaching compels students to ask not just "What have I learned?" but also "Who am I becoming?" Education is always about priorities. The call of teaching is for those who seek first to serve students.

Transformational teaching works because it is focused on individual potential. It has a significant effect on learning. Slavich and Zimbardo (2012, p. 570) report that "several well-controlled studies have now shown that students demonstrate more learning, better conceptual understanding, superior class attendance, greater persistence, and increased engagement when collaborative or interactive teaching methods are used compared to when traditional lecturing is employed" (Armbruster et al., 2009; Armstrong et al., 2007; Dahlgren et al., 2005; Deslauriers et al., 2011; Freeman et al., 2007; Haak et al., 2011; and more!).

The act of teaching is one of this world's most interesting phenomena because it is saturated with familiarity, which upon further examination shows a rather unfamiliar complexity. We think we know good teaching when we see or experience it, but when we look at whether learning has occurred, we might have our doubts. Not unlike politics or religion, we all have an opinion whether informed or not about how the best teachers teach. Familiarity with teaching can be bedrock experience but it also can breed malpractice. Experience is good for context but not necessarily for a foundation in decision-making about the quality of pedagogy.

Myths of Pedagogy

Jerome Bruner was a pioneer in educational psychology who built a comprehensive model of pedagogy focused on how our minds work, how people learn, and how teachers should teach. He (1996) writes about *folk pedagogy*, a set of assumptions that laypersons and educators construct based on their own intuitive theories. Bruner calls them myths, half-truths, and convenient fiction. Rather than rejecting them outright, he suggests we build upon them with good theory and research to guide practice. I offered a table of Ten Myths and Facts of Pedagogy (2003) as an effort to apply Bruner's suggestion that we can learn from the contrast between pedagogical fact and fiction (Table 0.1). Here is a revised version of the ten myths with ten corresponding facts based on research and best practice.

Notice that all the myths and facts in the table involve teaching and learning at the classroom level. I have limited my focus to pedagogy because of the vitality and essentialness of the teacher–student dynamic in education. Teachers can make a difference by crafting learning environments that prioritize their students.

Table 0.1 Ten Myths and Facts of Pedagogy

Myths	Facts
Blank stares and bovine-like eyes on students' faces are inevitable and unavoidable: all teachers should expect to see them.	Human curiosity is inborn but often stifled by school practices. Curiosity can be nurtured and rekindled if learners are viewed as active agents in need of support from teachers and peers.
Lectures, even well-planned ones, dampen enthusiasm for learning.	Exposition in its many forms can be immensely beneficial. Students by definition are novices who lack knowledge; however, great lecturers are few.
Effective teaching occurs in direct proportion to time on task.	The quantity of time spent on learning content and skills is an unreliable variable in itself. Time is an important element in learning, but the key to effective teaching is the quality of engagement with the subject matter by the learner.
Teaching someone something adds to their storehouse of knowledge.	Teaching is more than presenting someone with something new. Teaching occurs when learning happens. Learning results when students are engaged in new and meaningful learning environments.
Tests contribute to the learning process because they show what students have learned.	Exams and quizzes hold students accountable and can provide feedback that reinforces learning. However, learning is only demonstrated when students apply new knowledge in different contexts.
The best teachers are those with a reputation for being hard.	Rigor is not productive when it means excessive and irrelevant requirements for learners. Rigor is good when it challenges students to their maximum potential. Learners need that hope.
Teachers with a reputation for making learning "fun" have sacrificed rigorous standards.	The best teachers connect to emotion as a basic human structure, finding ways to incorporate joy in learning.
Technological advances in this century demonstrate how less than essential teachers are.	Students need teachers' assistance in learning. The process of learning requires the organization, insightful challenges, feedback, and motivation provided by good teachers. Technology can assist but is not a substitute for teacher–student relationships.

(Continued)

Table 0.1 (Continued)

Myths	Facts
Covering subject matter connected to rigorous standards is the most vital role of teachers.	Teaching for coverage is vastly overrated and mostly irrelevant. Teachers build their identity by serving many roles, and deserve recognition for their individual expertise.
High quality core-standards produce more learning.	High standards are important but readiness to learn is essential. Foisting rigorous grade-level learning standards on students can frustrate learning. Developing "strategic learning qualities" in students promotes life-long learning.

Source: "Debunk these 10 myths about teaching and learning" by T. Rosebrough in *The Teaching Professor*.
Copyright 2003 by Magna Publications. Adapted with permission.

Organization of this Book

The subsequent chapters in this book elaborate upon and analyze the ten myths and facts in the above table. Each numbered myth and fact and thus each chapter does not depend upon a sequence; so, after the "Introduction" readers can choose the chapter wherein to start: beginning, middle, or end, based on their interests. I am hopeful that this synthesis of contrasting ideas in pedagogy will serve teachers and leaders well in looking for deeper insight into our discipline of education and specifically into teaching for transformational learning.

In the writing you will notice "Perspectives" illustrated with a lightbulb. Each "Perspective" is meant to enlighten and inspire further insight. The goal is to provide clarity, inspiration, application, and undevrstanding throughout this book. Also, after each chapter is a section called, "Final Thoughts." This section briefly summarizes that particular chapter.

1

Nurturing Curiosity

Myth # 1	Fact # 1
Blank stares and bovine-like eyes on students' faces are inevitable and unavoidable: All teachers should expect to see them.	Human curiosity is inborn but often stifled by school practices. Curiosity can be nurtured and rekindled if learners are viewed as active agents in need of support from teachers and peers.

We are born curious but schools have a tendency to ignore this attribution, even to slowly but surely "school" it out of us. We teachers are sometimes certain that our learners can only be motivated by snappy lectures and fast-paced media. It is not so much "Thall shall not be bored" for students as "Thou shall not slow me down" for teachers that becomes the mantra of contemporary educators who enter the classroom expecting "bovine-like eyes," especially in this era of pacing guides. How we perceive our students is a fundamental principle of pedagogy. Times change but the essence of what makes us human does not change.

Part of our humanness is curiosity and with it comes questions. The best teachers have always asked and encouraged questions. We teach with questions. Ostroff (2016) says that "questions are curiosity writ large. . . The act of asking them activates the prefrontal cortex, also known as the critical thinking part of the brain" (pp. 107–108). Questions are best when coming from students themselves, with wise teachers encouraging them with leading questions to explore and discuss. Some teachers with standards to meet often think they have no time for questions beyond what the standards suggest. This hesitation is especially true in the primary grades where teachers often think their students lack discussive abilities.

Perspective: Inquiry with Young Learners

We sometimes suffer from low expectations regarding inquiry with young learners. Questions with primary students are a matter of patience and expectation. Most young children are bursting with curiosity. It is even more vital with young children to listen carefully to their comments and questions, and then build teacher questions on their individual thoughts. It is quite simple and intuitive, and enjoyable to experience their insatiable curiosity. We can have the standards in the back of our minds as we interact. This way we are using the standards and they are not using us. The point is that in the end their questions are more important than the teacher's. This is true of all learners but especially young ones.

Freedom from Fear

Part of the effort to increase student motivation to learn is realizing that students have a human need to take charge of their own lives, to grow and fulfill their potential. Psychologists call this need *self-determination*. Posey (2019) cites self-determination theory in her description of human curiosity, that the motivation for learning comes from wanting to satisfy a curiosity. Some writers use the term *agency* as a synonym for self-determination. Students seem to have a basic need for self-determination, and when teachers support their autonomy, competence, and relatedness (their need to be social, to feel loved), it enhances their ability to learn. It is an intrinsic motivation.

Ormrod (2019) echoes that we want a sense of *autonomy* in what we do, and a real freedom of *choice* (within reasonable limits) in the activities in which we engage. Note that this way of thinking, this cognitive theory, is the opposite of behavioral theory that says humans need reinforcement with rewards for motivation to learn.

Perspective: How We See Our Students

Teaching to human curiosity as a concept is not new. As Dallas Willard (1998) observed, it is a uniquely modern notion to teach subject matter that may not have an effect on human lives. Educators are here to change lives, to inspire students to want to learn throughout their lives. Old practices are often best practices. Smart phones, social media, and artificial intelligence are wondrously new to this century, but also serve as addictive traps, representing a behavioral conditioning phenomenon. Their omnipresence, however, should not convince educators to compete with them or to blame them for our students' blank stares. How we see our students and consequently how we set our goals should guide how we relate and what pedagogical processes we choose. In a phrase, we should respect the learner.

To fully respect learners we have to earn their trust. Teachers serve in role of not only authority but of real power. Students have every right to feel some fear in the dynamic of the teacher–student relationship. Here is where we teachers often underestimate our power. Here is also where the role of teacher–relater is critical. Relating to students is easier for some teachers than others because of their personality—these teachers must be intentional, even self-conscious in not taking for granted how they relate to students. Teachers who are not so naturally "social" simply have to work more deliberately on their empathy and communication skills. (Relationship skills and habits are addressed in Chapter 8.)

For either teacher personality-type as a relater, that teacher must realize that *fear* puts students' natural curiosity at risk. Curiosity when encouraged leads to errors which engender fear. When students are fearful (Reeves, 2021) is when they most need to trust their teachers. Transformational learning can occur when students break through the bounds of their fears. Curriculum which stimulates trial-and-error learning with a trusted teacher allows for a kind of controlled floundering (sometimes termed productive struggle) with learners. An environment of rigor combined with trust creates positive emotions.

Thomas Armstrong (Rebora, 2019) discusses how high school curriculum needs to be more affective for teens, especially if our attention to rigorous academic and intellectual work diminishes our desire to stimulate curiosity. Looking at the academic only can actually diminish our kindling of curiosity. We must be attuned to the social and spiritual "to be more engaging in terms of humor, vitality, joy, and even negative emotions like strong opinions and anger, to bring out those qualities and channel them, so that they aren't expressed in dangerous ways outside of school" (pp. 25–26). Curriculum in the hands of attentive teachers can connect to distracted, despairing, and disadvantaged students.

Perspective: Watching the Clock

One of my memories as a student, especially in the middle school years, was watching the big round clock up on the wall of my last period class. The school exit bell always rang at 3:17 p.m. The minute hand on that clock did not move smoothly but clicked from hash mark to hash mark. I liked school overall but could not wait to go home to my parents and friends. I was blessed to have a stable home life to return to everyday. Many students watch similar school clocks with a totally different feeling. They despair that the clicking minute hand is going to force them out of their safe haven of school into a turbulent home life and neighborhood. Informed empathy, a sense of not only caring for but knowing our students, is a beginning of respecting our learners.

Respect includes knowing learners and the process of teaching them. Perhaps the term, "respect the learner," does not go far enough.

Revering Students

We can revere students by "revering teaching." A. G. Rud and Jim Garrison (2012), without saccharine-tinged sentimentality, write about *reverence* as a "largely forgotten virtue in American society. When we do remember it, we usually confine it narrowly to the religious domain and assume that the separation of church and state necessitates that we ignore it, at least in public schools" (p. 1). The authors refer to contributors in their book who realize that:

> Good teaching involves forming character, molding destinies, creating an enduring passion for learning, appreciating beauty, respecting silence, caring for others, and much more. In some sense, teaching is spiritual, although not necessarily a religious, activity. When done well, it paves the way for human sociability and intimacy and allows teachers to find creative self-expression in the classroom community.
>
> (p. 1)

The ancient Rhetoricians valued changing learners by engaging them with tools of contrast, repetition, aphorisms, questions, and analogy. The teachings of Confucius, the dialogues of Plato, and parables of Jesus evidenced these concepts of engagement. The goal of the ancients was never to simply impart meaningless or irrelevant information removed from society and the human condition. All three of these teachers, although different in methodology, centered on transforming their learners and improving society.

Roth (2024) writes about the history of *students* across the ages, highlighting how the means and purposes of education changed with Confucius, Socrates, Jesus, and in this century, Sal Khan. It is interesting to compare the pedagogical purposes of the four to see how each perceives his students. Everything flows from how we see the learner learning, and we have a discipline in educational psychology which focuses on the nature of learning, analyzing how students learn. It is one of the three P's of the discipline of education: psychology (who), philosophy (why), and pedagogy (how). As we describe famous educators' approaches across the ages we must contextualize them within their culture.

Confucius lived in ancient China in chaotic times. His pedagogy was strongly didactic and focused on helping students become self-determining moral citizens serving society with good will and benevolence. We can still find many of his platitudes on school and college building walls, etched in stone for all to view. Thomas Lickona's modern school ethics (1991) of knowing the good, desiring the good, and doing the good are quite harmonious with Confucian thinking. Confucius saw the teacher's role as traditional in teaching five core values: benevolence, righteousness, propriety, wisdom, and fidelity.

Socrates was also quite traditional but approached his 469 B.C. Greek students with questions for them to deduce "truth," to critically analyze a difficult subject and lead students to self-illumination. We often think of the Socratic method as free-flowing interaction with students prioritized in the process. The opposite is true: While there is teacher–student interaction with student questions encouraged (pointedly so), there is also an overriding focus on the subject matter at hand with the teacher leading them through intellectual curiosity to one correct answer, often highlighting student ignorance. Like Confucius, Socrates played the role of teacher not just guiding but directing a closed-ended questioning process in a tight structure.

Jesus not only began modern time, he transformed teaching. In the Gospels, we see a master teacher at his craft. In Matthew 13, for example, we can find ancient rhetorical devices like the use of metaphors, similes, repetition, contrast, aphorisms, and questions. (We modernists should note the presence of brain-based principles as well.) We find a brilliant effort to connect his purposes to what his learners already knew through the use of one of the best teaching tools ever utilized: *stories*. Theologians may want to cast him as a traditional teacher sitting on a mount and sermonizing (which he did), but educators can look for something else: Precise, learner-centered pedagogy which connected and challenged at the same time. Above all, he knew his students.

All three of these teachers centered on transforming their learners and improving society. Aspects of their pedagogy like the power of stories are just as relevant today.

Perspective: Humpty Dumpty Got Back Up

Nancy Broyles (2018) relates how reading and writing about a nursery rhyme can change how students interact with one another and their world. She cites author Dan Santat's book (Roaring Brooks Press, 2017), *After the Fall: How Humpty Dumpty Got Back Up Again*, where Humpty tells his own story about what happens next after the infamous fall. The beauty of the story retold is the

> moral for students: They can fall and get back up and treat the moment as just that, a momentary setback. It is all here: Contrast of a retold story; Repetition of a familiar rhyme; Analogy in the metaphor of resiliently climbing after a fall. And there can be driving questions that probe like, "Humpty Dumpty was afraid of falling again, but he managed to climb the wall anyway. How did motivation apply here?" (p. 73). There is a lesson that allows the teacher to evaluate impact. The resilience to succeed after intermittent failure is a life lesson found even in a nursery rhyme if we look for it.

Sal Khan belongs strongly to this century. With his background in technology and business, he is the prototype for what many policymakers view as today's educator. Khan created the Khan Academy channel on YouTube which currently has 8.17 million subscribers. The Academy's videos have been viewed more than 2 billion times. Khan created this platform to compensate for what he perceived as the failings of old-school, traditional approaches to teaching and learning.

His educational videos are intended to accelerate learning by freeing teachers from spending time on lectures and giving them more time for interaction with students, sometimes called a "flipped classroom." Khan's latest innovation is generative artificial intelligence (AI) called "Khanmigo" where teachers and students work together using AI tutorials, even allowing AI to write first drafts of term papers. His idea is to inspire students to manage their own process of learning through inquiry at their own pace. Teams of students work together to apply their knowledge. In terms of exciting (and fearful) moments for technology, AI at the very least can be compared to the impactful introduction of the internet and smartphones. AI likely will, in terms of change in education, be revolutionary.

Diliberti et al. (2024) surveyed a national sample of 1020 teachers in fall 2023. Of these K–12 teachers, 18% reported using AI for teaching with another 15% attempting AI at least once. They found that middle school and high school language arts and social studies teachers were more likely to use AI. The most common AI tools used were adapting instructional content to fit the level of their students and to generate materials. Educators are finding that AI tools are quite valuable in synthesizing and summarizing content. Leaders reported that 60% of their districts were ramping up training for AI use. The motivation reported was the "potential for AI to make teachers' jobs easier" (p. 2).

A Common Flaw

While teachers in some settings have comparably the most stressful jobs of any professional, the salient question of course is not just about assisting teachers but whether AI will help students learn. The risk here is limiting the role of a real live teacher, although it seems that many leaders think that technology should play the central role even to the point of terming it "personalized learning." Computers can relegate teachers to the role of teaching assistants if care is not taken to build a positive, human classroom environment. Good intentions are not enough in building effective learning environments, as we learned with No Child Left Behind and its teaching-to-the-test mentality. The Khan Academy concept has advantages in its automated efficiency, but efficiency has long been overrated in schooling. We can resist complacency and especially mindlessness in allowing ourselves to be bound by contemporary thinking.

Perspective: Mindlessness

Mindlessness is a human process of giving away our agency, our unique ability to think for ourselves with moral courage. Context is essential, which leads us to a bit of history. Horace Mann's concept of graded schools, borrowed from the Prussians, is based on chronological age to replace one-room schoolhouses in the 19th century, and seems a necessary organizational efficiency for many reasons. Graded schooling's predecessor, the one-room schoolhouse, had a vertical grouping concept that surprisingly worked well because the teacher and students were forced to adapt to individual differences. Older students actually served as teaching assistants in many one-room schools, creating a kind of cross-pollination in learning. One-room schools worked! But the sheer number of students streaming into schools because of "free" public education changed the dynamic of organization, necessitating horizontally grouped graded schools in the United States. Grade 1—six-year olds and grade 2—seven-year olds worked well as long as teachers were sensitive to the individual differences of their students within the chronological age groupings.

Inevitably, large achievement gaps began to sprout among students of the same age in our graded schools and such gaps only increased as time rolled on. The point here is individual human attributes must be considered (readiness) and planned for by sensitive, reflective, and *mindful* educators whatever the era and whatever the classroom organizational culture.

Standardized schools and the idea of graded schools share a common flaw. People *assume* if we set high standards, require teachers to rigidly teach to them, and then test students annually that we will achieve not only accountability but eventually good outcomes. People over many years *assumed* by teaching students of the same age grade by grade the same subjects that we would achieve homogenously good outcomes. Assumptions are often flawed and mindless because they lack balance.

Perspective: Life in the Balance

Educators in our current era are definitely conflicted. Some show frustration and even disgust with anything we cannot measure—these educators have bought into standardized learning. Many others fear the individualized tech-oriented approach that some call personalization. Alfie Kohn (2015) calls it "behaviorism on a screen," where children are stuck in front of a computer for hours as instruction is individualized for them. Most of us know, whether we are teachers or not, that life is found in the balance of instructing young people *and* allowing them to accept responsibility for their learning. For schools to conduct the education of our children in ways that are extreme and counter to this principle of balance is short-sighted and even catastrophic for young learners.

We do not need computers to personalize education, although if used with sensitivity, they can assist tremendously in diagnosis and organization. Fred Ende (2019) gives us the personal part of personalized learning. He reflects that several teachers helped him with life—to become who he is—in three ways:

1. Investing in relationships (allowed him to keep his identity while also growing it)
2. Connecting learning to love (they helped him in his loneliness)

3. Convincing him there is no limit to learning (they steadied his desire to grow)

Who we are involves innate curiosity. Connecting to it helps us fully become who we are. Because curiosity is already built into our nature as learners, teachers who wish to transform learners often have to get out of their own way. In other words, to stimulate curiosity we have to avoid ways of killing it. Curiosity begets creativity, and standardization is the enemy of creativity. Odileke (2024) lists some simple steps to connect to curiosity, by avoiding:

1. Excessive test preparation—find a balance between test prep and nurturing a love for learning.
2. Lecture-heavy instruction—stop spoon-feeding of information and allow exploration of ideas by students with smart question-based strategies.
3. Overreliance on computer programs—balance screen time with authentic, hands-on learning.
4. Disconnection from students' lives—use required curriculum as a platform for seeking relevant and meaningful learning through open-ended questions. (pp. 2–3)

Teachers make the difference when learners are viewed as active agents in need of support from them and other students, nurturing curiosity and other human gifts in students. Students like young Fred Ende need the life changing environment that comes with classrooms that enrich human curiosity. The learners in our classrooms are uniquely created with differing needs but common attributes. Changing times need not change timeless approaches to pedagogy that are attuned to sparking curiosity in learners.

Final Thoughts

If we nurture curiosity in our students, they will defy the current malaise of expectations and demonstrate that they are active agents in learning. A luminous part of our humanness is our curiosity, and learners' questions reflect this inborn trait. The best questions come from students themselves with encouragement from wise teachers. Primary grade learners whose curiosity is perhaps burning brightest should be valued for their questions.

Learners seek self-determination or agency in their desire to take charge of their lives. They should be respected by teachers who revere teaching them. The history of students across the ages can be highlighted with the pedagogies of Confucius, Socrates, Jesus, and in this century, Sal Khan. The first three teachers from ancient eras centered on transformational learning. Khan's teaching reflects a more standardized approach through technology.

Teachers can connect to learners' curiosity by navigation of the bounds of excessive testing with more personalized instruction, avoiding over-reliance upon exposition, seeking a balance between hands-on efforts and the benefits of technology, and launching more student-centered pedagogy in response to required core curriculum. Transformational learning emanates from investing in relationships, compassionate teaching, and communicating that all students can aspire to learning without limits, without fear.

Standardization in education unbalances classroom environments with its fixed, predictable tenor and practices. Balance is called for in pedagogy to inspire the curious with creative teaching. By using the Transformational Pedagogy Model, teachers return to the roots of holism. Transformational teachers are needed to foster transformational learning.

Holism means smart *and* caring teachers. Why would we settle for less when such teachers deliver? They deliver high achievement, invite curiosity, and promote creativity. In a word, they *transform*.

2

Embracing Lecture

Myth # 2	Fact # 2
Lectures, even well-planned ones, dampen enthusiasm for learning.	Exposition in its many forms can be immensely beneficial. Students by definition are novices who lack knowledge; however, great lecturers are few.

In 1450, Johannes Gutenberg unveiled his working prototype of a moveable type printing press, with Bibles rolling off the press in 1454, portending a tenuous place for lecturing in school classrooms where learners could otherwise have their own reading material. Professors in medieval universities as well as teachers in cathedral schools in previous centuries usually possessed the only manuscripts; so, not only were there no required texts, but also the students were expected to listen and take notes for hours at a time. The teachers' lectures were a mix of reading and talking from a manuscript behind a lectern.

Years since, instead of less traditional lecturing after the advent of the printing press, there has been a stubborn cling to exposition as the primary teaching mode in six subsequent centuries through even today's digital age. Why such persistence?

One word twice: tradition, tradition. Lectures are teachers' inherited and customary behavior. Lecturing occupies a comfort zone for many teachers.

With pedagogical practices we have a strong tendency to imitate what we have experienced, and most educators have had teachers who lectured a lot. Another reason we still rely upon exposition is that it is easier to implement—teachers can know the material and it seems efficient as per time on task to just go talk about it. A third reason is likely psychological: Many teachers got into the profession because their egos warm to the control aspect of sage-on-the-stage. They did not hear Mark Twain say that if teaching were the same as telling we would all be so smart that we could not stand ourselves!

Anyone who has had the privilege of an education has experienced teachers who are great lecturers. We remember them because they not only spoke well, but they also broke down the subject material into coherent parts and then put them back together again. They likely crafted stories and employed humor. With lectures, learners are placed in a more passive role as listeners and watchers in a kind of unconscious priming, not for the best lead-in to in-depth learning (Gazzaniga, 2001). This is not to say lecture-hearers do not learn—it can be a form of learning akin to a nature walk where we see and hear things that arouse enough curiosity to return to our house and research what we observed.

Perspective: The Art of Lecture

What is the best lecture you ever heard? The best lecturer? For me it was Dr. Cohn in a biology course in my second year of college. His subject was the human body. It was a course where I actually read the text material before his lectures because I wanted to listen with some intelligent thoughts. He was that good: A calm, smooth, humorous, motivating, authoritative presence, with lots of eye contact and strategic use of overhead transparencies (just as good as PowerPoint in his hands). I had a very good high school class in biology that focused on the plant and animal kingdoms in a survey manner. But in college I was ready for more depth as we learned about all the systems of the human body: circulatory, excretory, nervous, etc. The teacher connected with me. I was in awe of what he taught and I learned. Since that course I have always read health articles with curiosity and listened to my doctor carefully!

Lecturers do connect sometimes in in-depth ways depending on the experience and motivation of the listeners. A frequent problem is that most students have not read the subject material before the lecture, but a good lecture can motivate learners to read post hoc. In other words, previous knowledge was activated, much like Piaget (1969) described the dynamic of assimilation and accommodation in the brain. We add to our schema units of knowledge in the brain by making them more sophisticated. In essence, this is constructivism where new ideas and ways of thinking build upon old ones. The "plasticity" of the brain allows it to adapt and change as it is given new experiences through our senses. The optimism of nurture as compared to nature is present here, which is Jean Piaget's original contribution to "growth theory," that we learn by interacting physically with objects and socially with others.

Great lectures connect to our emotions, and brain-based learning theory has a prominent place for the role of emotion. Posey (2019) writes how teachers create the social-emotional climate of a classroom that can either enhance or inhibit learning with individual learners. That is, our brains assign value and meaning to sensory input based on our prior experiences through emotion networks.

All Good Lectures Are Emotional

A "dry" lecture means no emotional connection occurred. Psychologist Carl Jung was right when he said, "There can be no transforming of darkness into light and of apathy into movement without emotion" (1938, p. 32). And, poet and writer Maya Angelou shared that "I've learned that people will forget what you said, people will forget what you did, but people will never forget how you made them feel." Great talks warm our feelings and teach us.

Lectures also connect through analysis and synthesis. The skill of analysis in particular is the hallmark of most teachers because so many of us got into teaching because we thought, "I can say that better than so and so. Why doesn't he explain it this or that way so we all can understand what he is trying to say?" We use analysis to focus on the parts of the whole, to understand its components.

Analysis is teaching from whole to parts, which is the most common strategy utilized. We as teachers have a compelling need to break down a concept into pieces so that learners can understand it—an important teaching skill. Break out the details and students will see how simple the concept is. Caution is needed here, however, as our intuitive thinking about analysis can lead us astray.

Digging Deeper

Teaching with synthesis may be more effective. Synthesis might begin with the parts enumerated, but its focus is on forming them into a whole. Perhaps our task in a class is introducing photosynthesis. Creating a big picture is saying, "Plants use a process called photosynthesis to make food for humans and animals. It is an amazing conversion of light energy from the sun using green chlorophyll which is contained in the plant." The word "simple" is important because we want to connect to learners' experience with green plants, food, and sunlight. A graphic or simple picture of a green plant like corn can accompany the introduction. Then come the smaller parts of analysis including water uptake, carbon dioxide intake, and the conversion of light into the chemical energy of glucose. Oxygen is released as a byproduct. This way-too-succinct analysis of the photosynthetic process can conclude with putting all the parts together in a synthesis directly related to our students as humans: "Notice how vital green plants are in taking in the carbon dioxide we exhale and releasing the oxygen we inhale. We depend on them just as they depend on us." Good lectures utilize both analysis and synthesis.

Synthesis is a process of combining the parts, not breaking them out. Brain-based teaching research and learning science (Bransford et al., 2000; Sawyer, 2006; Posey, 2019) say that most of us understand new concepts when teachers proceed from general to specific with deduction. We do best when we introduce the subject generally before describing specifics. Why? One big reason is that we are more likely to connect to the prior knowledge of our learners. Taking our time with the "big picture" is important because context is a learning structure we create for the learner. It can be a theme or an idea that provides a broader framework within which learning can fit. Have you ever tried to tell a joke without a contextual segue? Nobody laughs! If learning "fits," it has meaning.

Perspective: Review and Preview

A simple discipline to follow in the classroom related to context is to briefly preview the day's objectives and/or content to be presented. It is also a sound principle to review the previous class's activities or goals met. All review and preview can be accomplished in a matter of a few minutes. Students can then "fit in" the knowledge they are expected to learn for that day as well as perceive the flow of knowledge communicated between classes. It is like walking into a big picture of a more complex understanding. Our goal with synthesis is to understand the whole.

Types of exposition are the lecture in its individual forms like the formal lecture from notes/PowerPoint; the interactive lecture (some call it conversational lecture) where teachers are strongly scripted but talk *with* their students as much as talking *to* them; a formal presentation where students are not expected to interact; a film or video presented as pertinent material support for the subject at hand; and a guest speaker who comes in, presents, and leaves after offering a different perspective on the subject at hand. Note that types of lecture mostly differ in degree not intent, that all have the goal of passing along information from teacher to student. Interactive lectures have the highest degree of student engagement and effectiveness in learning.

A Caveat: Seeking Variety and Holism

If we stay with exposition as our primary pedagogy, we run the risk of skipping opportunities for holism in teaching roles. As seen in the "Transformational Pedagogy Model" in the Introduction, transformational teachers are holistic in that they aspire to playing three roles: scholar, practitioner, and relater. They also plan for three goal sets: academic, social, and spiritual. If we view learners as holistic in their needs, we teachers must aspire to the whole as well. The lecture method likely will eclipse the relater role as compared to the roles of scholar and practitioner, especially if the lecture is a more formal one dominated by teacher talk. Teachers who are good at lecturing do project caring, but the relater role can be inhibited by too much teacher-talk.

The relater role will be explored in some depth later in this book, but the evidence is that students learn more easily if they perceive the teacher as caring about them and respectful of their individual identities. In fact, the work of Frey et al. (2019) asserts that *all* learning is socio-emotional. We who lecture must caution ourselves not to glide along without stopping to project care for students as individuals. We are not lecturing to a class; we are lecturing to individual learners. The relater role is meant to conjoin with our scholar and practitioner roles.

Perspective: Touring Life

If synergizing all three roles is so desirable, why don't more teachers model it? With some teachers it is likely obstinacy, an attitude born out of both pride and ignorance. They have not thought through what school is about. With others the reluctance to move forward comes from fear—fear of changing the way we have always taught. This fear is very real because all of us fear failure. And, yes, with some other teachers, they are just coasting. Good teaching begins with attitude. Simply playing out the days as though we are on a tour bus looking out on the learner-landscape is not best practice or good mental health promotion, and it affects students negatively. The insight and compassion of a transformational teacher begins by getting off the bus and living life through our students' eyes.

Using a variety of methods increases the probability of reaching out to and engaging students. If we want to teach the values of character, for example, we must relate to our students. Relaters put the care in character education. The graphic tool of a continuum is a metaphor for contrast and placement of ideas, specifically in this chapter on "embracing lecture" as a pedagogy. (Chapter 10 highlights other more student-centered pedagogies.)

Figure 2.1 is a "Continuum of Teaching Strategies" (a horizontal line) with Exposition on the right side of the line, Discussion at the center of the line, and Inquiry on the left. Two arrows sit above the center of the Continuum (line): One points to the right and is labeled Subject-Centered teaching; the second arrow points to the left and is labeled Student-Centered teaching.

Continuum of Teaching Strategies

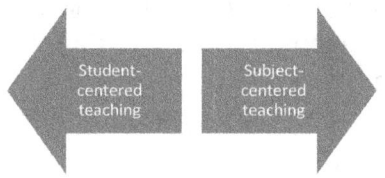

Inquiry **Discussion** **Exposition**

Figure 2.1 Continuum of Teaching Strategies.

All teachers can place what they do in classrooms at particular times at some point on the above continuum. The mystery lies not in where but why, and as stated before, "why we teach equals who we teach." The type of pedagogy that we use should depend on our students as they seek to connect with a curriculum. Of course a teacher-scholar's knowledge of the curriculum is crucial—confidence in and love of our subject is foundational. Teachers can be seen as a mediator, a conduit, or even a translator between the subject/curriculum and their learners, with the task divided between the two roles of practitioner and relater. The relater role is vital here because we need sensitivity and insight into learner needs. Thus, the relater role can influence how we choose to teach in the practitioner role.

Our students are novices while teachers are experts who know their subject so well that they can determine how best to translate it to learners who "do not speak that language." Knowledge can be like a code that needs to be broken to be understood. We teachers must know something! About our subject. About how to teach it. About whom we are teaching. Bruner (paraphrased) brilliantly said that any subject can be taught to students at any level if their teachers offer it to them at their readiness level. When we say that all students can learn we mean they are simply ignorant not stupid. They lack knowledge and great teachers to inspire them to want to know.

Walk into most any classroom especially above middle childhood and we will likely find pedagogy from the right side of the continuum, with lecture being the primary method (I use the term "exposition" because it is the more inclusive concept). This fact is not so much an indictment as it is a reality of survival and tradition, survival because exposition seems less risky in terms of teacher control, and tradition because it is the most familiar mode.

The salient point: Inhabiting one side of the continuum habitually is not good pedagogy, reflecting a teacher who is not likely to connect with and engage students over time. This concern applies to either side of the continuum, inquiry (student-centered learning) on the left or exposition (teacher-centered learning) on the right. Variety in pedagogy contains an element of appropriateness, but also of novelty, the spice of learning. Todays' public schools seem to emphasize traditional conformity over novelty.

Traditional teachers are more subject-centered and value exposition more highly. They act upon their belief that teaching's main purpose is to pass along an academic and social heritage. They likely view students as more passive in the classroom, with teachers as experts and students as novices (which is accurate). The caveat here is that passive learning is an oxymoron. Learning occurs in the brain when one neuron connects to another. With a good lecture, our brain cells do not just sit there like couch potatoes when learning is occurring. I like to think of the connection as one neuron talking persuasively to another neuron. Persuasion involves a reason to learn, and a good lecture can create that rationale, especially lecture that intentionally involves and encourages interaction with students.

Interactive Lecture

All teachers can learn to deliver a lecture in a conversational manner, what Schmoker (2018) and others (Silver et al., 2007; Marzano, 2009) call interactive lecture. By its name we can infer that this pedagogy combines exposition and discussion. When we properly monitor and connect it to required reading and writing, interactive lecture is effective. As Schmoker says, "the teaching is still both *intellectually active and interactive:* students frequently take notes, work in pairs, and complete problems and quick-writes throughout the lesson" (p. 98). There is student participation. The bonus is that this template "will meet the demands of any standardized test" (p. 98), as it adequately prepares students for their college and/or career paths.

Marzano (2009) is particularly assertive, saying interactive lecture "*dramatically increases* students' understanding of new information across content areas and at every grade level" (p. 87), especially if teachers regularly monitor student understanding. Schmoker emphasizes that teachers should revisit or even reteach subject matter if students are confused about the content. How do we know they are confused or do not understand? We ask them questions at regular intervals throughout the lecture time; and, we pay attention to the questions they ask as well! The questions that students ask as well as their comments are like platinum because they tell us whether they are learning. All we need to do as teachers is listen.

What Matters to Teachers

As we discuss a place for lecture in our teaching, it is instructive to ask, "What matters in pedagogy? What do we really want to achieve? What are the ends of our schooling?" We in education like to critique our schools and our teachers, but as we know, education mirrors the needs of society even if the reflection is uneven and blurry at times. The world of work must weigh in.

McTighe and Willis (2019) highlighted the value of what employers look for in college graduates in the annual National

Association of Colleges and Employers survey. While the world of work is not the ultimate value in education goals (despite what policymakers seem to think), it is certainly instructive and important to know what employers want. The 2018 version posits strong writing skills, public speaking, a team mentality, a high grade point average, relevant work experience, critical thinking and problem solving skills, attention to detail, and leadership experience. This skill set is a reasonably good example of the relative holism (team mentality, leadership experience) and depth (strong writing, critical thinking) of the world's challenges! But, it is to be compared to other goals, as we shall see, that are richer, deeper, artistic, and scientific.

> **Perspective: Why We Teach=Who We Teach**
>
> The desired end of our teaching can take many forms. Some look at the world of work, some at academic standards, some (actually many) at simply the next grade level, and some at more transcendent values. No doubt today's students face new demands from society, demands that we cannot even foresee at present. These demands should force us to confront anew why we teach. Someone asks us, "Oh, you're a teacher. What do you teach?" And, our automatic answer is, "I teach fifth grade." Well, we do, but a stronger answer is, "I teach fifth graders." Secondary teachers say, "Biology," when the more thoughtful (and research-based) response might be, "I teach students biology." Semantics, maybe or maybe not. By focusing on learners first we can set more inclusive parameters: We can meet holistic needs *and* the goals of deeper academic understanding. For transformational teachers, why=who.

How can we shift from the excesses and omissions of the present? How can we move to an age of transformational teaching and learning? We must be skeptical. We should question our purpose and process in teaching. Students must feel or perceive a personal connection between their ability and motivation to learn and their teacher's presentation of curriculum. Elementary school principal, Sabrina, comments on purpose and personalization in teaching:

> In a world where state testing dictates teacher effectiveness, a school's grade, and often community perception,

it can be difficult to remember the purpose of education is not assessment. To me the purpose of education is to prepare students to be successful in life. It is to provide students with an opportunity to develop the skills (social, emotional, and academic) they need for life. *The purpose of education is opportunity* (italics added). Education changes the trajectory for students. It pulls them from poverty, gives them hope for a better future, develops character, and inspires students to reach their full potential. The purpose of education is to help students realize their ultimate purpose in life and provide them with the knowledge to fulfill their purpose in life. Education should change a child's life regardless of their socioeconomic background. Affluent and low-income students alike should be held to high expectations, be given tools that motivate them, and push them to think critically.

Preparing students for a successful life deserves our focus and attention as reflective practitioners. Our academic discipline is Education, which means that we have to confront the challenges of educational philosophy, psychology, and pedagogy in a variety of settings. Philosophy is the beginning—it tells us why we teach and who we are as professionals. Psychology is deeply human—it tells us whom we teach and how learners learn. Pedagogy is our unique challenge—it is how well we teach, which can be simple in concept but challenging to fulfill. In simplicity, we can find profundity.

Knowing why we teach is a beginning. Various purposes for teaching are embraced by educators. One purpose is to teach so that rigorous content is learned. Another is to teach so that creative minds can be stimulated. Yet another is to teach so that social-emotional needs of learners are met. Are all our learners getting these *opportunities*? John Dewey (1938) philosophized that great teaching embraces a "continuity of experience," learning that continues for a lifetime.

Meeting this worthy goal requires the flexibility of thought to place ourselves with frequency on many points on the teaching strategies continuum. Only our wills and wisdom can make this happen.

Final Thoughts

Lectures do not have to "dampen enthusiasm for learning." The lecture is one of the forms of exposition as shown on the "Continuum of Teaching Strategies" in this chapter. A lecture in its classic form with a teacher speaking from an outline or notes with little to no student interaction is a difficult "connect" to make for most teachers. Great lecturers are few, but most of us remember teachers who not only spoke well but coherently with reasonable analysis and synthesis. Great lectures can reach our emotions.

Besides the formal lecture, other forms of exposition include conversational lectures where more discussion is scripted, film or video, and guest speakers who come in and present to offer perhaps a different perspective on the subject at hand. Lecture as a concept overall can risk missing opportunities for holism synergized in the three teaching roles evidenced in the Transformational Pedagogy Model presented in the Introduction. Thus, the overuse of lecture in our classrooms is not best practice, but the interactive lecture can be a highly effective and efficient means toward the goal of transformational learning. Strategies for questioning, inquiry, and discussion, which are a vital part of interactive lecturing, are presented in Chapters 3 and 10.

The "Continuum of Teaching Strategies" demonstrates that good teachers should inhabit many points on the continuum, including various types of inquiry and discussion. Variety in pedagogy is one of the hallmarks of a transformational teacher. The interactive lecture can encourage transformational learning because students are intellectually active and interactive with peers. The goal of teaching to create life-long learners is a worthy one, requiring flexibility of thought across any continuum of pedagogies.

3

Engaging Learners

Myth # 3	Fact # 3
Effective teaching occurs in direct proportion to time on task.	The quantity of time spent on learning content and skills is an unreliable variable in itself. Time is an important element in learning, but the key to effective teaching is the quality of engagement with the subject matter by the learner.

Time and engagement are related, but only in how we spend the time we have, not how much. Few topics in education have been studied more extensively than time on task over the last 60 years. In a meta-analysis, Godwin et al. (2021) chronicle research efforts since 1963 to study learning outcomes related to time on task. Their conclusion is that "the relationship between time and learning remains elusive as prior research has obtained mixed findings." They say, "It is possible not all tasks are equally beneficial for learning and thus the relationship between time and learning may not be uniform across tasks" (p. 2). The results can only be termed as mixed as to a positive association between time spent on-task and achievement.

Carvalho et al. (2017) concluded that time on task showed mixed benefits, with age as a variable. The quantity of time spent by adults on assignments preparing for exams was a significant predictor: They were more likely to obtain higher scores. However, time spent on preparation for the exams did not translate into equal learning benefits. Hence, the relationship between time and learning is not a reliable variable, giving credence to the quality of learning activities as a significant variable. Karweit and Slavin (1981) studied elementary age students on this topic and found that *how* they actually used the time was a better predictor of achievement. The overriding conclusion seems to focus on individual students' connection to the learning at hand. Time alone is a poor predictor of learning.

This work is significant in that large swaths of public schools have reduced time on physical education, art, music, and recreation and increased academic subject time with expectations of higher achievement on test scores. A perfect storm of intensive academic focus has been combined with test-prep classrooms across the United States.

Perspective: May Day!

If time is an important variable in education, there certainly is less free nonacademic time, except for the month of May after annual testing is concluded. In many school systems across the United States, the month of May is wasted academic time. The teaching-to-the-test burden is lifted and students watch films, enjoy outdoor activities, and take field trips (unrelated to any tested academic goals). We might ask, "Where is the parental outrage?" Interestingly, a PDK Poll (2019) taken pre-COVID-19 shows 83% of K–12 parents support teachers having more flexibility. It is unlikely that today's busy parents realize that the only time of flexibility for many teachers comes after the annual testing ritual.

To engage students in any curriculum, teachers need the flexibility of time to create inspiration and motivation so that students can be "effortful" and "strategic." Effortful means hard-working and strategic means focused. There are likely two reasons that public outcry has not evidenced in the United States over teaching-to-the-test schooling (the "4 t's"). One reason is that *on the surface* it is difficult to argue against high standards and annual testing. Most everyone understands that the education of our young people should be based on high expectations, and that learners should be held accountable for their learning. Savvy educators and parents know, however, that merely promoting "high standards with accountability" in a federal/state sound-bite argument does not equate to a good education for students. Rather, it is what good teachers are allowed to do within a system of high expectations that matters.

The second reason is that most annual standardized exams are not tests for promotion to the next grade level. And, if they are in some places, the minimum pass rate is set so low, as in Massachusetts at 40% on the English test, 25% on the math, and 30% on biology, with retesting allowed up to four more times, that parents are not too concerned. Interestingly, the Massachusetts Comprehensive Assessment System (MCAS) test (which is a graduation exam) in Massachusetts was voted out in 2024 after 30 years, despite the state hovering around the top spot in NAEP rankings each year (Lederman, 2024). The tide may be turning in some places against the extremity of equating test scores with learning as the public perceives "curriculum narrowing" and the inevitable discrimination against disadvantaged children.

A sense of balance is needed in the quest to soften the rigid and impersonal effects of standardization. Students need teachers who have freedom to teach. I might stipulate here that while freedom to teach can exist within mandated content, the culture or context of the school and classroom affects everything and everyone, including the ability to create and respond to learner needs. Teachers from experience know that engagement is related to student agency within school structures of high expectations. It is vital to define the reality of education by seeking context. Policymakers (and unfortunately parents) usually operate well above the reality of teachers' teaching students each day. The best way to find context is to use comparison, which in itself is an important teaching tool. I turn from this "tyranny of the present" to a historical metaphor.

Why We Teach

In a remarkable historical novel set at the battle of Gettysburg during the American Civil War, Michael Shaara in *The Killer Angels* (1975) narrates a scene centered on Colonel Joshua Lawrence Chamberlain, leader of the 20th Maine Regiment. Mr. Chamberlain was professor of rhetoric at Bowdoin College before enlisting and receiving a commission to serve with the Maine Volunteers. One week before Gettysburg in late June 1863, Chamberlain was given command of the Regiment which now stood at 250 men from what began as 1000 the previous fall.

Colonel Chamberlain is awakened after a wearisome march (80 miles in 4 days of the hottest weather he had ever known) to be told that he was now to include in his command 120 mutinous men from the old Second Maine. He had a crisis. Their enlistment had run out for their Regiment and they were all sent home, except these 120 who had foolishly signed 3-year papers thinking they would fight on with their same group from Maine. All of them had been stripped of their rifles, threatened with court-martial, and force-marched without food the night before meeting Chamberlain. His orders were to shoot any man who refused to do his duty. What could he do? He was not about to shoot anyone, especially men from his home state of Maine. How could he even guard them, given the quickly changing circumstances of an impending battle? What could he say to these men who were fatigued, discouraged, extremely suspicious of authority, and feeling betrayed in their call?

First he ordered them fed. (No one who is hungry listens very well.) Then he listened privately to their spokesman share their grievances. (The "privately" part is strongly effective in educational studies on motivation.) Afterward, almost embarrassingly, Chamberlain gathers them together and began by telling them who he is, where he is from, and what is left of his Regiment. (He is frank, honest, caring, and seeks to identify with them.) He then sums up *why* all of them are there, saying,

Some came in mainly because we were bored at home and this looked like it might be fun. Some came because we were ashamed not to. Many of us came . . . because it was the right thing to do. All of us have seen men die. Many of us never saw a black man back home. We think on that, too. But freedom . . . is not just a word . . . But we're here for something new. I don't . . . . This hasn't happened much in the history of the world. We're an army going out to set other men free . . . What we are all fighting for, in the end, is each other.

(pp. 29–30)

Then he concludes by defining reality:

Well, this is still the army, but you're as free as I can make you. Go ahead and talk for a while. If you want your rifles for this fight you'll have them back and nothing else will be said. If you won't join us you'll come along under guard. When this is over I'll do what I can to see that you get fair treatment. Now we have to move out.

(p. 31)

Moments later the whole force was to press on toward Gettysburg, the bloody battle that changed the momentum of the Civil War toward the Union. Chamberlain had now turned away from what was transpiring behind him with these demoralized men. All but six had asked for their rifles and were forming their ranks with their new Regiment, the 20th. This band of men in a few days, against all odds, held a hill called "Little Round Top" to win the most strategic "skirmish" of the most decisive battle of the Civil War. Chamberlain survived the war as a brigadier general and went on to become a four-term governor of Maine and president of Bowdoin College.

Gettysburg is a U.S. martial milestone along with Washington's crossing of the Delaware and D-Day on Normandy Beach. While education is hardly a battle scene from Gettysburg, it is a battlefield in the first three decades of this century for why we are teaching and how we are teaching, affecting millions of lives. Leadership that prioritizes the needs of students marches us in the right direction.

Do we leaders know that education is about students? What do we say to teachers who are "fatigued, discouraged, extremely suspicious of authority, and feeling betrayed in their call?" Many just want to go home like the 120 soldiers. How do we inspire them to pick up their proverbial rifles to fight on? How did the colonel view the men who served under him? Notice that Lawrence Chamberlain did not objectify or talk down to the ones he hoped would join him. Can we leaders define reality for teachers? Can we empathize with teachers and students? Do we know why teachers "joined up?" Do all teachers know that we embody leadership when we respect our learners? We as educators to lead must inspire. But inspiration is ineffective unless we challenge as well.

Who Taught You?

Teaching is the essential profession. As Willard reminds us (1998), everyone on this earth who does anything has had a teacher in some capacity. So who taught you? Someone did. *Those who teach affect eternity*, wrote historian Henry Adams, underlining our calling, our privilege, and our responsibility. The reasons we chose this profession might vary somewhat, but most any teacher can respond quickly when asked why. We all know the classic three reasons why some teachers chose education for their career: June, July, and August. All right, so now in most places, given school calendars, there are only two: June and July. (All teachers NEED the summer break.) Just like, unfortunately, it is quite possible that folks in the three-now-two-reasons group also conform to the old dictum of "Don't smile 'til Thanksgiving."

For most, thankfully, there are more transcendent reasons. For some they still embrace an old-fashioned yet still vital word: calling. For others, they seem to have known since childhood they wanted to be a teacher, often playing "teacher" at home. Perhaps a teacher inspired them when they were students. Some had parents who were teachers and were role models. Some want to help struggling or disadvantaged students because either they also struggled as a child or they saw a sibling or friend who was disadvantaged or they have seen inequity and want to be change-agents. And yes, many teacher-parents discourage their children from even considering the job—after all, education often feels like a war that is unwinnable. Why we are in the profession matters because of how teachers affect students, which is related to what we teach and how we teach, and most fundamentally, to how we view our learners.

Where are we now in U.S. education? While the simplicity of our motivation to inspire and create might have compelled us to enter the world of teaching, the stress of meeting the needs of students, parents, and state agencies can displace us from our comfort zones. Hopefully some say . . . we have "powered" our way in many states through an educational era of test scores holding primacy over kids. But wait. Some schools and districts have achieved higher scores from teaching-to-the-test. Is there regret if we leave the 4t's behind?

It seems safe to say, "Not really," for the record number of teachers leaving the profession, even before the COVID-19 pandemic (Hackman & Morath, 2018), at the fastest rate since 2001. "The educators may be finding new jobs at other schools, or leaving education altogether: The departures come alongside protests in six states where teachers in some cases shut down schools over tight budgets, small raises and poor conditions" (p. 1). The authors write about teachers who say that students are not valued and education is not prioritized in this country. Small salaries are just one symptom of this lack of priority.

A more recent, post-COVID-19 study (Brown, 2025) from the University of Missouri found

> that 78% of teachers have thought about quitting since the COVID pandemic. The study revealed that it's not just new teachers . . . but seasoned educators with more than five years of experience who are even more likely to want out.
>
> (p. 1)

Even educators with strong coping skills report high levels of stress, especially from feeling unsupported, low pay, and student misbehavior.

Teacher preparation enrollment is so low that state legislatures are funding teacher scholarships in online programs at the baccalaureate level in an urgent (and desperate) effort to attract new teachers. In other words, policymakers are trying to fix a problem they created. So what about good teachers who are holding on? One teacher who wants to stay with the profession says she wants to help her district as well as state and national decision-makers understand that

> these are children whom we are teaching. It's vital to take care of them and guide them to learn in a way that is relevant instead of cramming in as much as possible. As cliché as it sounds, these kids are our future. I worry sometimes about the kinds of humans that they'll grow up to be.

How we view our students makes a difference. Again, context is vital—we have to know what matters to our students. They desperately want authority figures who will persevere and believe in them. Cara, a high school teacher, writes poignantly about one bad day and her desire to teach to transform:

> Today was a tough day. Lots of fights and drama at school. We haven't had a day like today in a long while. But after all got quiet, it circled back around for me--the need for teaching the whole child. My school has so many damaged children, coming from a range of situations and all levels of trauma. Traumas both seen and unseen, but all directly affecting my students. But then I step back for my inner pragmatist to come out and say, of course they can't accept that type of teaching, or most teaching for that matter. If we look at what Maslow says, if we believe there is a hierarchy of needs, and if we agree that children can't learn at the higher levels if their basic physiological needs are not being met, then how do we reach these kids that don't have the basics? The students who don't know where they are going to sleep

that night or if there will be food to eat that day. Young teens that are asked to take on adult responsibilities--students that deal with so much trauma they don't know a life without it. I had a conversation with one of my students this week about why teachers want to teach. And I think most teachers want to be transformational teachers. But so many of us face the challenge of how to teach if the children are not set up to learn from the beginning.

Educators have little control over the challenges facing the students they teach, yet the screws of accountability have been tightened as though they have. Our schools over the last dozen years or so have been forced to swallow a milky, unappetizing solution that does not match the problem. Cara, in her story of one bad day, sums up teachers' hopes as well as school and society's problems. If many of our children "are not set up to learn," we are charged in the schools to provide a learning environment that will support their needs and consequently the schools' needs. If basic needs are met, it may be as simple as answering the question, "Why should I learn this?" with curriculum and processes that build in choice and autonomy, which is what transformation is about.

Perspective: Student Conferencing

Students have always asked, "Why should I learn this?" whether audibly or not. Imagine a simple way to connect with and engage students even in this standardized age of schooling. Try an old idea that really personalizes learning: student conferences. Kristen Cove (2025) gives many reasons why we should set aside time regularly to meet one-to-one with learners: (1) Connection and building relationships as we learn more about whom we are teaching—family, likes and dislikes, dreams and passions, what they find easy and what they see as challenging. (2) When students begin to know their teachers care about them they are much more willing to ask questions, meaning they will become more open and vulnerable. (3) Learners want to please teachers and are more motivated to do better. (4) Student conferencing leads to deeper learning because differentiation becomes more natural. Teachers are more aware of their learners' fears, feelings, and limitations. (5) Assessing students is easier because we know agreed-upon goals, where the struggles are, and where to look for change. All grades can benefit, but K–8 are likely the most fruitful/manageable years to set aside time for conference meetings. Set aside an hour

> at a time or whatever works. Meetings can range 3–10 minutes per student every 2 weeks, taking a day to a day and a half total for all depending on class size. Take notes, keep records, and remind students what they are to work on. Cove reports, "much to my delight, conferencing resulted in high interest on the topic we were covering, a sense of relatability to the student and their work, a much deeper understanding" (p. 5) for teacher and student. It is not a sacrifice of time—conferencing pays forward because engagement actually saves time! Some conferences will take longer, some will be very short. We teachers must lead.

Some may feel, understandably, they cannot spare the time organizing student conferences—which is taking a private minute or two daily to interact individually. To ask how students are doing can impact achievement, and lives. Transformational learning emanates from prioritizing students, and the most student-centered process for engaging learners is the strategic use of questions (even in student conferences). The most useful tool we have as teachers is the question, and the use of questions can be found at every point on our "Continuum of Teaching Strategies" presented earlier in Chapter 2, from Exposition to Discussion to Inquiry. We can think of questions this way: Every good conversation we have had in life has likely been prompted by a question. The use of questions comes in many forms.

Questioning and Engagement

It is a reality that time for questions and responses in today's schools is limited by the need to move on to the next standard. Time spent well on questioning pedagogies, however, pays immense dividends on achievement. All effective pedagogies are undergirded by a vital dynamo: good questions.

First, it is important to discuss the quality of questions themselves. Krajcik and Shin (2014) in their discussion of Project-Based Learning say that the hallmark of PBL is a "driving question that guides interaction" (p. 281). They cite Krajcik and Czerniak (2013) who say that good driving questions have several features. Their context is elementary and middle grades science, but their features of good questions apply to all disciplines or subject areas. The features include:

1. *Feasible* so that learners can actually answer the questions.
2. *Worthwhile* in that they contain rich curriculum content, reflecting what scientists (or historians or mathematicians or writers) actually do.
3. *Contextualized* in the real world and important.
4. *Meaningful* in that they are interesting to students.
5. *Ethical* in that they do no harm to individuals, organisms, or the environment. (p. 281)

The authors (p. 282) list a couple of engaging questions in science: "Why do some things stop while others keep going?" which is set in a physics classroom concerning the transfer and transformation of energy. And, "How can you prevent your good friends from getting sick?" which is situated in a biology classroom studying cells, systems, microbiology, and disease.

Orlich et al. (2007) add further dimension to the use of questions. They discuss "multiple–response questions" designed for three or four students to respond. Their example: "Where might Christopher Columbus have landed if he had set sail from London (instead of Spain) and headed due west" (p. 238)? These type of questions are the opposite of more closed, sequential questions that teachers often use in recitation periods.

There are some "default habits" we teachers resort to out of convenience, habits to avoid, like repeating the question when no one seems to answer; or answering the question ourselves in a fit of impatience; or going back to a favorite student for desired responses; or simply not listening well to our students. All of these habits, what Orlich et al. call "idiosyncrasies," emanate from our lack of not only patience but investment in teacher-led discussions. Student "talk" is gold in transformational learning. It is where educators can diagnose if or when change is happening as a result of our efforts. The gold is tarnished, however, if time constraints are permitted to dominate our pedagogy.

Good questions and their attending techniques have been studied and written about often. The classic description of questions can be matched with the cognitive domain of Benjamin Bloom's taxonomy (Bloom, 1956). The taxonomy is hierarchical in that it builds in complexity from basic knowledge to evaluative questions:

1. Knowledge—knows facts, concepts, symbols
2. Comprehension—understands meanings
3. Application—transfers knowledge to new settings
4. Analysis—reduces complex issues to simpler components
5. Synthesis—blends older ideas into novel or creative uses
6. Evaluation—generates criteria for judging

Arthur Costa (1991) provided a useful, condensed version of Bloom's levels of thinking/questioning by organizing 1–2 into Input, 3–4 into Process, and 5–6 into Output. His emphasis on action verbs in each category is valuable, for example, Input: recall, define, name; Process: analyze, organize, construct; Output: conclude, criticize, create. Also, Norman Webb (1997) (Webb et al., 2023) gave us a framework for Depth of Knowledge designed to establish context with four levels: Recall and Reproduction, Skills and Concepts, Strategic Thinking, and Extended Thinking. The intent is to create a common language for engaging students.

Seminally, here are a few notes on Bloom's list: *Application* should be teachers' "apple of the eye" in discussions and formative evaluation. When learning is demonstrated to move or transfer from one setting to another (real world or conceptual), we know that our efforts to "teach" are successful. For example, we teach decimal fractions along with percentages in upper elementary and middle school. We demonstrate the process of converting a common fraction to a decimal fraction like .25 and then to a percentage like 25% (move decimal point two places to the right and add the percent sign). We ask, "What is the common fraction equivalent to .25 and 25%?" Good students say, "25/100" and we say, "Can you reduce that to a common fraction in its simplest form?" If students learned their common fractions well, they say, "1/4" and we say, "Correct. How did you reduce it?" All of the above questions and answers are *knowledge* and *comprehension*-based, which are vital algorithms to learn.

But then we ask, "What if you were in shoe store and a set of your expensive, highly valued sneakers are 25% off?" How do you figure the sale price? What if the sales tax is 9.075%? What is the final price on a pair of originally priced $150 shoes? All these questions are *application*-based because students must apply their knowledge to the real world of a shoe store.

Analysis questions play to the use of logic, which is the essence of critical thinking for our students. Teachers often must "force" the use of critical thinking because as learners we often resist the hard work involved. You could ask, "What are the steps or processes you must go through before you actually board a plane?" Analysis pulls things apart while synthesis puts them together.

Perspective: Creativity Doesn't Work in a Vacuum

Synthesis is special as a questioning technique because it asks learners to "put things together" or create. Creativity is taking disparate variables of the known and synthesizing them into something novel. In many ways, the goal of fostering creative thinking is the essence of transformational learning. Just for fun and edification, I went to Apple Safari and prompted the search engine—AI Overview—for an example of a creative question (retrieved December 2024): "If you could design a new planet to live on, what unique features would it have and how would life on that planet be different than Earth?" (I do not think this question is particularly original.) Notice that the question calls for some prior knowledge of our planet Earth, some analysis and synthesis, but asks for some imagination, too. Creativity does not work in a vacuum—it has to have some kind of knowledge upon which to build. From known to novel.

And finally, *evaluation* questions lead to ownership for learners. It is Bloom's ultimate prize in levels of thinking because such questions lead to a transformative mix of knowledge and personal engagement. For an example, we could simply extend the creative question and ask, "What do you like about planet Earth? Would you want to live on a different planet? Why?" Or, an American history question at the evaluation level: Mount

Rushmore in South Dakota has four consequential presidents carved in its hillside: George Washington, Thomas Jefferson, Abraham Lincoln, and Theodore Roosevelt, completed by the sculptor in 1941 after 14 years of cutting into the granite hill. What president would you add? Take down? Why? Answering these questions requires informed opinions, not just an opinion but a thoroughly informed one that can be defended. When we are engaged and informed at a high level, we can allow ourselves to buy into an idea (or a cause like the Gettysburg soldiers mentioned above). We as learners have been asked to evaluate knowledge and make it our own.

Awareness and Flow

While the taxonomy is often used in formulating objectives and evaluation instruments, here we are isolating the framework to questioning. Learners need a cognitive structure to organize information into knowledge and the taxonomy does just that if teachers have an *awareness*. Marzano et al. (2001) make the point that the taxonomy can help teachers decide what and how to teach as well as how to evaluate the effectiveness of what was taught.

Teachers at all levels struggle with using good questions to stimulate discussion and build knowledge. Most of our problems seem to stem from a lack of awareness of not only the complexity of our questions, but of where we want the interaction to lead (keeping a standard in mind helps). We have not planned our questions so that we know when we are "there."

Perspective: Destination

An old Johnny Hart B.C. comic strip features a bird riding on the back of a turtle en route to a destination. The bird complains about how slowly they are traveling, that they will never get where they're going. The turtle abruptly stops, says "that's it!" comes out of his shell, "runs" up a hill, looks over a valley, and "screeches" back down the hill. The bird asks for an explanation. The turtle says, "I was just making sure where we are going is still there."

Scripted questions can work in more structured learning situations, but as a general rule teachers do much better with interactive pedagogies when we just let the questions flow. In 2004, psychologist Mihaly Csikszentmihalyi gave a TED Talk on his concept of *flow*. He defined it by citing the words of artists, poets, scientists, and athletes who each had found themselves so engaged in their task, activity, or work that they achieved this psychological state. The most defining part of the psychologist's talk for me was when he detailed his research on how it feels to be in a state of flow:

1. We are completely into what we are doing, focused and concentrating.
2. There is a sense of ecstasy—of being outside everyday results.
3. We have great inner clarity—knowing what needs to be done, and how well we are doing.
4. We know the activity is doable—that our skills are adequate to the task.
5. There is a sense of serenity—we have no worries about ourselves, and a feeling going beyond the boundaries of the ego.
6. There is a sense of timelessness—we are thoroughly focused on the present and hours seem to pass by in a minute.
7. There is intrinsic motivation; whatever produces flow becomes its own reward.

We as teachers can have flow with questions by first having an awareness of taxonomies on our levels of thinking, and secondly a plan to meeting an objective or standard. At the simplest level, there is nothing wrong with using knowledge level questions if they help students toward higher level thinking and knowledge (Marzano, 2004; Orlich et al., 2007). In fact, knowledge and comprehension questions can elicit responses that build not only flow in the discussion, but also build confidence in the learner. Creativity (a higher level akin to synthesis) and evaluation (the highest level of complexity) do not happen without a foundation of knowledge.

Here I apply "flow" to using questions in a discussion, but when I read and hear Csikszentmihalyi's work I think in a larger sense of engaged learning, a kind of intense and perhaps infrequent kind of engagement, yet a seemingly ideal state of learning and doing. Perhaps my readers can recall a time in a classroom when they were in a state of flow. Strangely, and I must smile as I write this, I remember learning many of the fine points of grammar in writing in a high school sophomore English class. Even though grammar is hardly a "flow-worthy" topic for most, the teacher was knowledgeable and humorous. I liked the detail and organization of learning to put words together in sentences and paragraphs. (We even diagrammed sentences!) It was novel and worth knowing and intrinsically motivating for me. I liked knowing something useful about a very common life activity—writing. I was grateful to that teacher when I got to college. It was transformational learning for me.

When students are guided by sensitive and knowledgeable teachers to inquire about topics tied to core curricula, and are allowed to research (with caution, the internet awaits!) and interact with peers on those topics, they become engaged learners! No teaching method is more effective than one which asks students to own their learning and allows teachers to assess the impact. Learning in small groups is ideal.

A Brief Look at Small Group Instruction

A pedagogy like small group instruction enables learners to interact and engage with peers and the teacher in ways of socialization that may actually be rare opportunities for our more isolated adolescents. And, small group inquiry and discussion are ideal platforms for developing "Strategic Learning Qualities" (SLQs) that are process-oriented skills for life-long learning. That is, the SLQs (Rosebrough & Leverett, 2011) of *openness, skepticism, civility, persistence, imagination,* and *curiosity* are developed as the result of teachers' asking questions and allowing the timeless traits of cognition, motivation, and personal responsibility to grow. These personal qualities are the best kind of learning outcomes because they last a lifetime. I will explore small group instruction and SLQs in more depth in Chapter 10.

Here I should reiterate emphasis on the socialization value of small group discussion. Allowing students to talk in a focused, safe way in small groups under the guidance of a wise teacher is an extremely valuable format for socioemotional learning. Tragically, it seems a generation of students is not receiving enough opportunities to talk with each other in authority figure-guided settings.

Perspective: Mental Health

A study out of Reuters Health spanning 2007–2018 sadly found (Joseph, 2019) that suicidal thinking, severe depression, and rates of self-injury among U.S. college students more than doubled over less than a decade, particularly in the second half of the study. Note that this is a pre-COVID-19 longitudinal study which suggests that even before the pandemic our students were at risk. Co-author Jean Twenge in the *Journal of Adolescent Health* says, "It suggests that something is seriously wrong in the lives of young people and that whatever went wrong seemed to happen around 2012, or 2013." While the purpose of the study was not to find cause, the study co-author noted that smartphones and social media became common and rather socially "mandatory" around that time. More than 610,000 undergraduates participated in the survey, average age of 21, two-thirds female and almost three-quarters white. Smartphone use has been associated with poorer sleep quality, and fewer face-to-face interactions.

Any pedagogy that maximizes social interaction under the savvy guidance of teachers is a plus. Recent mental health findings are frightening. Nurturing, strategically smart, relational teachers are needed!

Final Thoughts

Educational research over the last 60 years seems conclusive: Time-on-task alone is a poor predictor of learning. Policymakers have created a perfect storm of intensive academic focus, annual testing tied to standards-based achievement and teacher accountability, and intentional lessening of "nonacademic time" in reducing and eliminating physical education, art, music, and recreation in schools. Time-on-task has become a metaphor for shackled teachers and disengaged students. Quantity is a poor substitute for quality if the goal is to transform learners.

If we seek to define reality in contemporary public schools, the conclusion is that educator and student agency are at a low ebb. Many teachers are fatigued, discouraged, suspicious of authority, and feeling betrayed. The victims overall are students. Educators need inspiration and hope in order to meet the myriad of challenges in their classrooms and hence society. A record number of teachers are leaving the profession because of perhaps the unintended consequences of standardized schooling: Teachers are less valued and students as individuals are not prioritized. COVID-19 has unearthed new stresses on top of the issues that flow from standardization in schooling. Teachers need less stress, not just tools to manage the stress they have.

Transformational learning as a goal can assist because it focuses on holistic potential. The most useful tool for engaging and transforming learners is the strategic use of questions. We can find the use of questions at every point on the "Continuum of Teaching Strategies" because every effective pedagogy requires them. Questions as a tool in teachers' toolboxes is vastly underrated in current times because of the pressure of core standards applied to "moving on."

The quality of questions and their attending techniques need a rebirth in our schools. Many teachers at all levels struggle with using good questions to stimulate discussion and build knowledge because of lack of awareness of the quality of their questions and lack of goal-setting in activities. The psychological concept of "flow" can be applied to discussions where sensitive and knowledgeable teachers can guide students to transformational learning.

A whole generation of students needs to regularly talk with each other and with teachers in small group discussions, away from the internet and smartphones. Socialization through quality goal-oriented interactions is urgently needed not only for life-long learning but good mental health.

4

Discovering How We Learn

Myth # 4	Fact # 4
Teaching someone something adds to their storehouse of knowledge.	Teaching is more than presenting someone with something new. Teaching occurs when learning happens. Learning results when students are engaged in new and meaningful learning environments.

Think of a huge warehouse where workers labor to bring in crates of materials to stack and store while also removing old boxes of storage to be destroyed or sold. Think now that this is *not* how our brains function. Neuroscience says our learning is not about addition and subtraction (although unused neurons do seem to wither and die), but about stimulus and connection. We also grow and lose connections throughout life.

Our brains (Jensen, 2005; Wolfe, 2010; Posey, 2019; Willis, 2024) are more like electrochemical factories where billions of neurons are present, waiting to be activated by sensory input from life experiences in rich learning environments, and also by the reflective interaction and connections within and between columns of neurons in the brain. Our brains are not storehouses for knowledge. Our brains are vibrant and wonderfully complex, integrated, and adaptable engines with nearly a million miles of nerve fibers stimulated by countless electrical and chemical charges made therein, as we as humans are being shaped and molded. Adaptability means brain plasticity, a reason for optimism in learning!

The chemicals are neurotransmitters, hormones, and peptides that facilitate connections between neurons. Classroom environments can be built and employed to use principles and encourage practices that support brain-compatible learning, which is the foundation of transformational learning. We might ask now, "What are we trying to transform?" My response and I suspect the response from most educators is the *whole person*. The essence of a good life is not necessarily knowing the right answers. It is knowing the right questions and finding peace as we consider the answers. Standardized education advocates ask, "How can we raise student achievement?" Their answer is to teach to core standards and test anything that moves. The difference between the two educational worldviews could not be more stark.

Teaching to transform the whole person involves mind, body, and spirit. Some associate the brain only with the cognitive and academic. They are emphatically wrong. If we seek to foster transformational learning, we must understand how the human brain learns and then teach to that conception, which is the epicenter of mind, body, and spirit. How does this conception relate to transformational learning?

How Our Brains Learn

It makes sense to teach to how we learn. Our brain is the visible part of the learning process, but it makes our mind, the invisible part, function. We teach to transform minds, what the ancients termed "heart and soul." When we teach to the whole child we teach to mind, heart, and soul. We make a tragic mistake in teaching only to the visible as we are called to teach to the invisible as well. The evidence is increasingly clear that our brain is wondrously made: It actually does grow new neurons and is adaptable to stress and novelty and emotional import. It even responds positively to physical exercise. In short, our minds are renewable and can be transformed! Surely this is educators' strongest and most growth-related "theory into practice" conceptual understanding. And, it all starts with brain-compatible thinking.

Here are six brain-compatible principles (Rosebrough & Leverett, 2011), which taken in sum, will show us how to teach to transform: repetition, challenge, novelty, meaning, feedback, and emotion. Resilient Children Need More Fun Every-day is an acronym for remembering the principles.

- ◆ Repetition: This factor is similar to feedback at least in the sense that it concerns the reinforcement of elements in the learning environment. Repetition is like practice, what educational psychologists call "rehearsal" (Gordon, 2006). Our brain cells need to acquire the ability to fire, and their ignition is tied to how often they have fired before. Thus, old-fashioned practice of a newly introduced concept is vital to learning the concept. For example, we can be introduced to the idea that multiplication is a shortcut to repeated addition, but we do not learn multiplication tables without repetitive use. Some students need more practice than others; hence, both nature and nurture are involved with the essence of repetition. Patricia Wolfe (2010) compares it to producing a well-trod path in a forest of neurons. The more repetition the more beaten the path. Students vary in their abilities but all lack experience in learning new concepts and ideas. Thus, teachers' repeating themselves at times or students' rehearsing by practicing a skill may seem redundant to some, but it is an essential principle for learning. Repetition with some dollops of novelty is good brain-learning. For example, teaching and training are different sides of the same coin, with the latter much narrower in conception. Training often involves a lot of repetition, but it is not the same as comprehensive teaching because it is so skill-specific, even if it can lead to learning. Memorizing is not the same thing as learning, but recalling something is the primary way teachers know students have learned. Memory seems like one part of the whole, a large part. Old-fashioned catechetical pedagogy has elements of brain-compatible learning, even though we have moved well past the ancient equating of memorization with learning (or have we in this age of standardization?). Some memory and recitation work can be a good thing.

Perspective: Memorization Trains the Brain

Memorizing and reciting lines from books and poems do have their place in contemporary schools. (We all know that foreign languages and computer science are fodder for the young of brain because of the repetitive process needed to learn the subjects.) The discipline of memorizing something could be likened to encoding a computer—it is a process of converting the targeted subject into receptive neurons in different parts of the brain by *repetition*. What is originally converted has to be retrieved and used (use it or lose it). Thus, recitation, usually vocal, is an integral part of memorization. Most of us have had the experience of a vendor's software sending us an "authentication" number to verify we really are us! It is a short memory quiz of a five or six-digit number—we can recall it without writing it down if we recite/repeat it softly to ourselves. We all know that we learn more than we demonstrate, or to say it another way: we do not necessarily show what we know. Younger brains have great plasticity for memorizing material with the attendant benefit of vocabulary-building. Many of us still remember portions of pieces we memorized like the "Gettysburg Address," "Paul Revere's Ride," the "Preamble to the Constitution" and more (part of the "more" for me were lines from Poe's "The Raven"). There is a discipline to learning something from memory that trains the brain to learn; and, it is best to take advantage of this discipline with young students. The caveat here is not to think conceptually of memorizing as the same thing as learning, but realizing that it can play an important role, an appropriate part of our overall pedagogy.

♦ Challenge: Challenge is vital—too little or too much and students are, respectively, bored or frustrated. Challenge with sprinkles of teacher sensitivity can be embedded in problems or good questions at most any school age. Problem solving must be a way of classroom life if we want to grow young brains. By age 12, students are ready for complex abstractions found in good literature, in mathematics, in science with an emphasis on allowing curious questions and topical research. The corpus callosum, the major bridge between our left and right brain hemispheres, is fully matured around age 12 and can carry 4 billion messages a second. Adolescent and adult brains are ready for extra challenges. Surprisingly, neural growth happens (Jensen, 2005; Jensen & McConchie, 2020) because of the process, not the solution. Appropriately challenging curriculum develops the brain, creating learning even in the midst of errors if presented in safe, stimulating, and supportive school environments.

- Novelty: An enriched learning environment is primary where we must expect more than drill-and-kill worksheets. Our brains perform a kind of neural customizing according to the learning environment, be it barren or be it a rich landscape of knowledge. Marian Diamond's famous experiments on the brains of rats at University of California, Los Angeles in the late 1960s showed that rats in an enriched environment with toys and physical challenges actually grew brains with thicker cortex, more dendrite branching, and larger cell bodies. Novelty is vital—physical things and social aspects must seem new and interesting, like putting new words to a favorite old melody. If something seems new it gets our attention. Just as the act of learning itself is new by definition, our brains and indeed our minds seek renewal. Collaborative groups, for example, do two important things that can seem novel: They impart valuing and caring (releasing good peptides), and they provide specific feedback for students on their ideas as well as their behaviors. Also, there is evidence that our brains may be designed for music and the arts. Liking a new song is stimulating—so is rediscovering an old favorite. Music actually primes the brain's neural pathways (Jensen, 2005). Listening to Mozart before a test can have a calming effect for optimum learning. Teachers are well served by changing things up in their classroom routines and pedagogy. It can be something as simple as a choral reading of a poem or as complex as planning a field trip. Or, we can plan an activity that requires physical movement and collaboration—it will seem new!

> **Perspective: A Novel Idea**
>
> After a unit study in western history, try this: Make a teacher-set of a dozen or so relevant dates-events on construction paper (event on front, date on back). For example, one for the Magna Carta-1215; one for the invention of an efficient moveable-type printing press-c. 1450; one for Luther's 95 theses-1517; one for the settling of Jamestown, VA-1607; one for the date of first African slaves brought to the English colonies-1619; one for the birth of Benjamin Franklin-1706 and/or George Washington-1732; one for the Declaration of U.S. Independence-1776 and other relevant dates-events. For student use on a second set, do not place the dates, just the events on another set of construction paper. Then ask a small group of (volunteer) students to consult with each other and stand up front of the class in chronologically order for the events. Let the rest of the class critique the small group's work. This activity leads to great interaction, an opportunity for learning civility, *and stresses history as chronology instead of dates to memorize* (although date memory often is collateral learning in this lesson because it is meaningful). Thus, even something as mundane as dates in history, with some imagination can become novel. Something that seems new to us as learners leads to an intrinsic motivation to engage and learn more effectively (Lepper et al., 2005; Wigfield et al., 2006).

- Meaning: Students must perceive relevancy in a curriculum if they are to learn anything. Schunk (2008) says that the brain's hippocampus plays a key role in consolidating information into knowledge. To reiterate, the hippocampus tells us who people are and the amygdala says whether we like them or not. Nonsense data is rejected or resisted by the brain. To teach eighth-grade students about World War II without reference to or context in their lives today is an example of nonsense or rote learning that will not be applied or remembered. The scourge of Naziism nearly covered the world in the first half of the 20th century. What did that mean? How is it still a relevant concern? Meaning comes from context and seems related to novelty and emotion as brain-principles.
- Feedback: We must work to eliminate threats when mistakes are made. It is a teacher's job to provide feedback—that is how students learn from their mistakes and successes. Feedback, even when critical must be positive; it must be presented in a supportive, growth

mindset environment. Love can be tough or demanding, but it must be love. No matter how many positives we add to our classroom environments, we must first work to reduce and eliminate the negatives. These include embarrassment, unrealistic deadlines, sarcasm, or lack of resources. Brain research tells us that fear and frustration can lead to a hopelessness in the learner that actually causes the brain to downshift in a physiological sense. Hormones like cortisol (Jensen, 2005; Jensen & McConchie, 2020; Wolfe, 2010; Posey, 2019) are released by the adrenal glands and have a depressing effect upon neural connections in the brain. Teachers are well served to distinguish between frustration and challenge by seeking to be sensitive to students as individuals as they provide feedback.

> **Perspective: Boiling it Down**
>
> If we think about and "boil it down" to a single (too simple) thought, teachers have one essential role: Providing feedback. We are the adults in the room generally; and, we as teacher-scholars have an absolute obligation to give all students "supportive correction." As novice-learners they rely upon us to indicate where they are right and where they are wrong. We can follow sage advice and put away the red pen and find a less divisive color. Correcting a paper is where our attitude is on display. This is no place for passive-aggressive educators! Are we constructive or are we destructive in the way we assess? For transformational learning, it is vital learners *feel* that their teachers want them to succeed, that errors are not fatal, and that they are being encouraged to learn.

♦ Emotions: Emotions are a key in learning. The amygdala, an almond-shaped gland in the middle of our brains, exerts a tremendous influence on our cortex. The brain, we are learning, craves information with emotional impact. We need emotional context for long-term memory to function. The amygdala processes our sensory information for its emotion (pleasure, pain, anger, sorrow, humor, nostalgia) and relays it to long-term memory. It is interesting (Jensen, 2005) to note that removing the brain's frontal lobe has little effect on intelligence test performance (even though it is the center for problem-solving); but removing the amygdala has a devastating effect upon our capacity for imagination, decision-making, creative play, humor, love, and music. Effective ways to teach to emotions include storytelling, role-playing, drama, art, music, debates, field trips, and guest speakers. Joy as an emotion in learning is explored in a later chapter, but transformational teachers habitually set something of a social-emotional table for learners.

Integrating the Elements

Perspective: Learning Is Complicated

I have a friend, Sam, who is no handyman but decided one day to replace all the doorknobs in his house. He and his wife were tired of looking at the outdated gold ones and wanted brushed nickel instead. Their budget was limited so the strategy was do-it-yourself (DIY). Sam hid his fear of failure and immediately visited YouTube for the DIY project of replacing doorknobs because this was all a new journey for him. With his newfound how-hard-could-it-be knowledge of installation, he then visited the hardware store to compare costs and styles of doorknobs. The store associate seemed knowledgeable and was willing to answer Sam's "dumb questions" about the task at hand. He learned that he needed a couple new tools. The cost of each knob was more than he expected, especially when he multiplied it times the number of doors (Sam had never realized they had so many) in his house. Sam decided to set aside time over the next two months to better afford the project and to relieve some of the pressure of what would be a trial-and-error process. He and his wife could live with half nickel and half gold knobs for a couple of months they thought. The first few replacements took longer than expected and required trips back and forth to the hardware store to acquire the correct knob model with bolt locks. The process got a bit easier after that, except when there were unexpected nuances like when Sam realized that an old knob had not been installed to measurement. Two months later the couple had brushed nickel knobs throughout their home, with every entry still accessible, and Sam, humbled but feeling accomplished, enjoyed his success thinking, "I can do more home projects myself" in the future.

The elements of Sam's learning are motivation, choice, exploration, questioning, trial-and-error, supportive environment, time, proper tools, and feeling successful. Strikingly, the brain-based principles are there, too: *Repetition* (lots of doorknobs to practice on); *Challenge* (Sam took on something he had never done before); *Novelty* (most of this DIY process was new to Sam); *Meaning* (he was motivated by choosing a challenge to do something he had never done but felt he could do, and yes, by saving money); *Feedback* (Sam could visually and audibly explore the installation using video, giving him confidence. He had a resource at the hardware store, an expert who could answer his questions); and *Emotion*—he felt the combination of his wife's support, reasonable time for completing the task, and the proper tools would lead to success. And, Sam's successful completion of his project made him feel good and confident about projects in the future. This is Dewey's "continuity of learning."

The latter is crucially important for wanting to continue to try and to learn. It is a life-long learning principle that transforms students into life-long learners. Without asserting that this vignette mimics a perfect learning environment, all the needed elements for learning are present in this handyman story. For me the standout learning elements are: Sam *chose* to take on the project while knowing encouraging support was present; he had the resources and tools needed; and *the time element and nature of the task were appropriate for his ability*, even as the work was challenging. "Dumb" questions seemed not only accepted but expected. Assessment is built in as an integral part of the project: The doorknobs had to work once installed. No one had to set goals for him. He was *self-motivated because the nature of the work interested and challenged him*. Success was his reward, not a score or grade. Neither YouTube nor the hardware guy would have been punished if Sam failed, but his succeeding likely portends future business for them.

When learning is prioritized over teaching, great teaching is enabled, transformational teaching. Learner success is a worthy goal that is often ignored as we put the cart (teacher and curriculum) before the horse (student). Successful learners assist us in defining good and bad teachers.

Perspective: What Is a Bad Teacher?

David Berliner (2018) says it simply and frankly: We have standardized accountability for teachers primarily because policymakers want to rid us of bad teachers. So what is a bad teacher? Berliner first says what is *not* a bad teacher:

> (1) one who is too strict or too permissive for an evaluator's taste; or (2) one that is using phonics while the principal believes in whole language, or vice versa; or (3) a teacher who is having a bad time because of a divorce or illness; or (4) teachers who aren't as confident in mathematics or science as we might want them to be.

Instead Berliner says by a bad teacher,

> I mean one who will hurt the children they teach. They will do this either by significantly retarding their progress, because the teacher has inadequate knowledge of what they teach; or they use methods, or hold attitudes that are harmful to some, or all of the children; or they have another job or difficult home life and cannot allocate the time needed to plan their classes adequately, nor muster the energy required to put in a proper days' work in a job that requires energy, empathy and continuous attention.

(pp. 4–5)

Notice that Berliner's description of a bad teacher includes lack of knowledge (nonscholar), poor methodology and work habits (nonpractitioner), and harmful relational attitudes (nonrelater). The gold standard in pedagogy and thus in learning is transformation. Inspiration from enthusiastic teachers should precede whatever relevant information is shared. Good questioning strategies should strategically undergird subject matter and problem solving. Teacher-relaters inspire intrinsic motivation to learn (Ormrod, 2012). The goal is transformation and is achieved by engaging the whole learner. Teachers have two enormous opportunities in regard to transforming learners. One is at the "micro" level, while the second is "macro" in concept.

Micro-Level Engagement

Teachers' first opportunity is to connect to the individual emotions of learners. We have evidence from neurological research (Frey et al.,

2019; Jensen, 2005; Jensen & McConchie, 2020; Posey, 2019) that engagement is tied to emotion. Teachers create the social-emotional climate of a classroom that can either enhance or inhibit learning with individual learners. That is, our brains assign value and meaning to sensory input based on our prior experiences through emotion networks. Learners through their natural curiosity are always asking, "Why do I want to know this?" To engage at the micro-level, we must Inspire, Question, and Relate. Inspiration from caring teachers affects the intellect and emotions. We must first *Inspire*. Inspiration is the power to move the intellect and emotions. And, we inspire through developmentally appropriate challenges.

Jean Piaget (1969) in simple terms identified the two sources of human learning. Learners learn from the sensory input of the physical world (books and printed material, nature, and mechanisms), and from the social world (adults and peers). Thus, knowledge is constructed when students find meaning with "objects and others." A "consolidation" process for long-term memory occurs in our brains through repetition and the application of meaning. Meaning comes from connections formed in our brains when teachers spark curiosity through inspiration. Teachers can initiate dissonance, can "situate" (Krajcik & Shin, 2014) learning in real-world contexts by inspiring inquisitive minds.

Perspective: Piaget's Process

Jean Piaget, a Swiss psychologist, was a hugely influential and significant figure in the exploration of how we learn. We know about his ages and stages of cognitive development, and about his biological-like principles of learning with assimilation, accommodation, and the state of cognitive balance called reflective equilibrium. He said we are driven by a constant striving for equilibrium between existing knowledge and new experiences. The constant striving part is dissonance brought on by *challenges*. What we may not know is how he arrived at many of his conclusions. Piaget broke all the rules and studied his own children over time (longitudinally). He gave them problems to solve and meticulously recorded what they said and did. He watched his children play! But, he gave them structure in their play so that he could more systematically observe and record. He synthesized all his observations and made predictions and conclusions concerning cognitive development. His research was ground-breaking in its method and its conclusions. Piaget explained to us how school children learn and when they learn. His theory is remarkably brain-compatible. He painted the cognitive landscape of how our students learn.

We must *Question*. Transformational teachers through their questions and through encouraging student-questions can drive curiosity. We can walk alongside our learners by asking questions that connect: Why is the sky blue? (Blue is the shortest wavelength of color in the prism of light, allowing it to be more strongly scattered by tiny air molecules. Violet is there, too, but our eyes see more energy from the sun as blue light.)

A vital part of transformational learning is the ability to *Relate*. Ormrod (2012) defines relatedness as a "fundamental need to feel socially connected and to secure the love and respect of others" (p. 441). Note the psychological contrast here. It's not just about me. It's you, too. The juxtaposition of relating and self-determining demonstrates as well as anything the complexity of human beings and their learning. Why don't we pay more attention to this dynamic in our schools and classrooms? This means that holistic teaching should be the norm, not the exception. Social-emotional learning is good brain science and must be conjoined with the intellect. Indeed, research shows that attention to the social-emotional facilitates academic learning (Frey et al., 2019; Durlack et al., 2011).

Perspective: Teacher–Student Relationships

School leader Christine shared how one student perceived her teacher amid the power of relationships. A student came to her frustrated with one of her teachers. The student felt that he (her teacher) didn't care anything about her and that she was having a difficult time paying attention in class. She requested a change of teachers. Coincidentally later that same day her teacher paid a visit and expressed concern about the student. All three were able to meet and have an honest discussion soon after that. The teacher–student relationship changed. She now knows her teacher cares and calls his history class one of her favorites. Christine says, "The power of emotional engaged learning is significant. When students know you care, it changes everything."

Macro-Level Opportunity

The second opportunity for transformational learning is more at the macro-level. Despite the ubiquity of outside accountability pressures, teachers are still uniquely able, with effort, to control and design their classroom learning environment. It is for teachers to decide on the proper amount of teacher control in their classroom (Orlich et al., 2007). In fashioning an engaging learning environment, they can create that brain-based big picture into which their students can walk. The validity of a positive yet challenging learning environment has been the fruitful focus of learning theorists from Piaget to Vygotsky to Bruner, and from Bandura to Darling-Hammond to Dweck. As Posey (2019) writes, "If the environment is supportive and safe for making mistakes, the brain contextualizes positive emotions for this interaction, and this will inform future motivation" (p. 40).

In a classroom where students *believe* their teachers want them to succeed they are more likely to work with persistence academically. As Ormrod (2012) relates, it is learners' perceptions of the classroom environment that affects their behavior. Not feeling fear of making mistakes in the process of learning is a huge factor in successful classroom environments. Willis (2024) writes that learning can sometimes be counterintuitive in that making mistakes en route to a correct answer is meaningful in improving memory. The learning environment matters in that students must feel more comfortable with peers, with lack of embarrassment a key reinforcement.

And, high-quality learning environments over time affect students' self-confidence and expectations for future success (Posey, 2019), an acquired trait known as *self-efficacy*. In such environments, students take charge of their own learning and behavior, quite the opposite of lock-step manipulated learning environments.

Perspective: Students Can Collaborate

Dina Strasser (2019) writes of creating classrooms for the "whole kid," saying that learning environments should build efficacy and agency:

> As a result, fruitful collaboration among students is not 'nice' for your kids to master before they make their own way in the world—it is absolutely necessary. It'sespecially necessary when problems get in the way of our goals. You know, like life. (p. 2.)

It is an expansion of the conception of student achievement to include encouraging learners to collaborate on classroom rules and management. It is teachers' controlling and designing their classroom environment to prioritize students and their learning.

Great teachers can still change lives even as the trend is the use of evaluation rubrics that often force a conformity to what state education officials deem good teaching. Sometimes this conforming-perception is wrong: Evaluation rubrics can offer flexibility if evaluators reward teachers who build in authenticity and creativity. Sometimes this perception is correct: Unwise evaluators focus almost exclusively on the academic because the test is looming at the end of each year. Like any environment, natural or human-made, we can observe and reflect about its quality. We pay attention to what is happening to us as teachers and to our students.

A high school history teacher shared that after more than a dozen years of teaching he had realized that transformation was more than trying a variety of pedagogies, whether his own or those imposed by his school district. He concluded that a social-emotional connection must be formed with his students prior to actually "teaching." He wanted an environment of student growth and success.

How we learn as a concept has long been deprioritized and often ignored not only by policymakers but by us in the education profession itself. It is time to change that.

Final Thoughts

In education, we make a mistake when we overshadow learning with a singular attention to teaching. Our priority as educators should be a constant refining and discovery of how people learn. Then, and only then, we can turn more logically to thinking about how we should teach. Despite standardized education's rather explicit drumbeat that learning is as simple as rigorous goals and accountability, how we learn is supremely complex. It is as complex as the human brain.

Our teaching to sync with how students learn obviously must be brain-compatible. Transformational learning involves mind, body, and spirit, and the epicenter of this transformation is holistically connecting to the human brain. Brain-compatible principles include repetition, challenge, novelty, meaning, feedback, and emotion. We should ask, "What are we trying to transform?" not, "How can we standardize education so that we can raise achievement?" The act of transforming learners will raise achievement as a byproduct of good teaching, and good teaching incorporates sound principles of brain-based elements. Aiming our efforts at achievement instead of academic/social/spiritual transformation misses the target. High test scores are a byproduct of transformational learning.

The goal is transformation and is achieved by engaging the whole learner. We teach at the micro-level by inspiring, questioning, and relating. We teach learners at the macro-level by designing classroom learning environments as rich, positive, safe, and supportive. Such environments affect the self-efficacy of learners who can then take charge of their own life-long learning behavior.

5

Testing, Testing

Myth # 5	Fact # 5
Tests contribute to the learning process because they show what students have learned.	Exams and quizzes hold students accountable and can provide feedback that reinforces learning. However, learning is only demonstrated when students apply new knowledge in different contexts.

The digital age is wondrous because of its accessibility to knowledge. Computers whether laptops, smartphones, or tablets are somewhat irresistible because they are personalized, speedy, and readily accessible. For education such technology is an opportunity for great benefit but it also carries a danger. We can consume "huge amounts of information divorced from purpose and meaning" (Rosebrough & Leverett, 2011, p. ix). This worldview is digital in essence, information divorced from the values of knowledge, and it is contagious with many powerbrokers when they discuss accountability. We know the drill, where we: Install high standards; require teachers to teach to them; force students annually to be tested for them; reward and punish educators and schools accordingly. We know this story well. How does the story end? Not happily ever after, as students and teachers absorb the impact.

Perspective: A Fox Tale

My doctoral chair, Alexander Frazier, in one of his many books, wrote in 1976 that "the chief nightmare of a mass society is that it will be unable to resist the drive toward standardization and conformity." The opposites of standardization and conformity are independence and creativity. Aesop's Fable about the Lion, Fox, and the Beasts applies. The Lion, being King of the Beasts, summoned animals to his cave to hear his last will and testament, claiming illness unto death. The Goat went in. The Sheep went in. And the Calf went in. The Fox, though invited, did not. Asked by the Lion, "Why did you not come in?" The Fox said, "I beg your Majesty's pardon, but I noticed the tracks of everyone going in but none coming out." Educators must be foxes, gracious and aware, but independent, not going into that cave.

Our discipline of education is a bit of a paradox. Other disciplines sometimes attack it because: (1) It is relatively new in its formation like sociology and psychology—John Dewey almost single-handedly created it at the turn of the 20th century; (2) It is an amalgam of other disciplines to some extent—my view is that its mix is a strength; and (3) People are so familiar with its function that contempt is easily bred. Education is a combination of philosophy, psychology, and pedagogy. The latter tenet, pedagogy, is pure and unfettered in classroom function and has been studied extensively for the past 100 years, with the research largely ignored in this century, hence the theme of this book. Philosophy and psychology are also a part of the discipline of education but they are academic domains in themselves as they are applied to the education of students. Philosophy means we start with knowing *why* we teach. Psychology means we know *who* learners are and thus how they learn.

Perspective: Education as a Discipline

I define our discipline here because testing and accountability are an indelible part of what we do if we want to be successful in pedagogy. As teachers we prepare (set goals); we instruct (choose good pedagogy); and we assess (we monitor and evaluate). The assessment must be tied to the goals in our preparation and not vice versa, as unfortunately, in tying our teaching to a test. Assessment or testing must not be the tail that wags the dog. Instead, our formative and summative assessments must assist us in knowing whether we are meeting our teaching goals. It is a critical difference.

To paraphrase the posting in the table at the top of this chapter: Tests can show some of what our students know, and they can motivate attention to learning. Asking "if this is going to be on the test" has always been a good question. But, learning is only really demonstrated when students apply their new knowledge in different contexts outside the classroom. Here I use psychology. Feedback, reinforcement, and accountability (which is a kind of feedback) are all indelible parts of learning. Our brains crave feedback as part of the cycle of neural development. What students demonstrate on a test should provide useful individual feedback that helps teachers adjust their instructional goals and strategies.

Using Test Results

Testing results should be primarily diagnostic in purpose, not trophies for show dogs at Westminster Kennel Club. John Hattie (2015) writes that we should be using assessment results for interpretive purposes not indicative ones. The "golden triad" in schooling is students, parents, and teachers sitting to interpret results together, and not just summative results. Assessment of course can demonstrate progress with annual exams, but if we are serious about tying evaluation to instructional goals, it is critical to use test information to inform teachers of their impact on students. It is simple diagnostics. Hattie stresses that it is reports not the tests that matter most to teachers. He says:

> Until we see tests as aids to enhance teaching and learning, and not primarily barometers of how much a student knows now, on this day, on this test, then developing more tests will add little, and will remain an expensive distraction. Educators need to understand what each student already knows, and where that student needs to go next in the teaching process.
>
> (p. 3)

He calls this "visible learning," and it is common sense for any teacher at any level who understands the process of teaching and learning. How can we transform the learning of students if their learning is not visible to their teachers in some way? Quite simply, we set goals, we instruct, we monitor our instruction, and we assess both formatively and summatively. Teachers need quality feedback from assessments, which do not have to be standardized exam dependent (although technology allows for incredibly detailed reports). But, Hattie further says:

> Why should teachers be asked to learn the language of measurement people? Instead, we measurement people should learn how to speak in the language of learning and teaching and provide interpretations that are in turn correctly interpreted by teachers, with consequential actions and decisions. Similarly we need reports from student assessments that help students understand their own progress in learning . . . but we need to stop the high-stakes methods and the overreliance on developing tests to maximize precision.
>
> (p. 4)

Focus must be on helping teachers to learn how they are impacting learning. A salient point here is that transformational learning can be found in the goals and instruction that we set up in the process. In many schools, supervisors visit classrooms often. What are they there to observe? One frustrated teacher says, "No matter how many observations I have in my room, they are only there to see data."

Given the discussion here of "visible learning," it is important when we walk into a classroom to ask, *How can we recognize transformational teaching and learning?* Following the "Transformational Pedagogy Model" (TPM), recognition hinges on the three basic components of education itself: curriculum, teacher, and students. A synergy must flow among the components:

- *Curriculum* is the content, the "what" of education. In the TPM, we find three goal structures: academic, social, and spiritual. Is the curriculum worth knowing in terms of importance, inspiration, challenge, and utility? Since no human can know everything there is to know, what knowledge has societal relevance and meaning? Does the knowledge have intellectual as well as import for social and individual spiritual growth? New and old information is a false dichotomy in that the new often rests upon the strength of the old. Curriculum-makers must choose wisely.

♦ *Teachers* bear a heavy mantle because we are the facilitators, the connectors, the translators between the curriculum and the students. In the TPM, we find three teacher-roles: scholar, practitioner, and relater. Are we well-prepared as whole teachers? Are we armed with sensitivity and creativity? Are we committed to meeting the learners where they are, and to where their potential lies? Do we know our students? Do we communicate caring?

♦ *Students* have a responsibility as well (which in contemporary education sometimes is lost). In the TPM, students are placed in the center of the model. To be transformed as learners, they must be engaged with a growth mindset to overcome obstacles and failings. Do they display a development of "Strategic Learning Qualities" (SLQs—detailed in Chapter 10) of openness, skepticism, persistence, civility, imagination, and curiosity? Are there opportunities for students to develop SLQs with inquiry and discussion?

If the goal is transformational learning, "formative interpretation" (Hattie's term) will tell teachers how to proceed in light of the "visible" progress or nonprogress. Overall, what do we want from our instruction if it is transformational? We desire learners who love to learn and will keep on learning for a lifetime. We desire students who learn about who they are and who begin to see their own potential as critical thinkers and compassionate people.

Perspective: What Did They Say?

Twenty years ago some fellow educators from around the state met with a state representative at the capitol who was sponsoring a bill on standardized testing. I asked him if he and his colleagues were considering the "whole child" in their deliberations on instruction and testing. He said, "I don't know what that is," without asking us to explain. A few years later I recall attending a meeting with State Department of Education officials who turned over the session to young MIT professionals to give a PowerPoint presentation on the critical nature of annual testing in our state. None of the measurement professionals had ever taught school, but they really knew tests and measurements. We walked away from the session as colleagues shaking our heads.

Policymakers who know little about education have seized authority from educators who know a lot about education. Policymakers view schooling from 20,000 feet. Teachers are at ground zero. We need to acknowledge and learn from ideas from above but educators must reclaim our schools. If students' learning in all its forms is prioritized, everybody wins. What should be our goal for learning? Transformational learning goes beyond showing knowledge on an annual test—this is the floor. The ceiling is the empowerment of our students toward application of knowledge, even toward student's learning how to learn, because learning is about application of knowledge in various contexts.

Learning Transfers

In reference to applying new knowledge in different contexts, educational psychologists use a term called *transfer* from the classroom. Transfer is a psychological concept essential to human functioning (Ormrod, 2012). We teach "assuming" that students will apply what they have learned to the outside world. Ormrod lists several factors that affect learning transfer, like meaningful and authentic learning transfer better, principles transfer better than facts, lots of examples and practice assist application, and that the less time the better between teaching a concept and application to a new context. Transfer to new places is how we demonstrate our learning.

Test results, not just the ubiquitous year-end exams but formative assessments as well, are best used as part of the learning process, especially in *authentic learning* where applications occur.

> **Perspective: Out There in Here**
>
> Authentic learning is a concept where teachers bring what's "out there" into classrooms. Learners can apply their knowledge in new contexts. It is intrinsically motivational for students because they immediately sense the relevance of the activity. For example, ask, "Your parents receive their utility bill each month. How is that calculated?" Discussion can then ensue about utility service workers whose job it is to read utility meters in yards and on houses (some are read with technology in some areas). Copy a real utility bill and study the usage table of water, gas, and electricity this month, last month, and last year. Look at the number readings—they are quite comprehensive! Do the math. Mathematics is used by local utility companies every month and by their customers. A good authentic math lesson on computation skills can follow (even flow) from a utility bill.

The Immeasurable

Our goals for teaching matter, which involves reflecting upon why we teach. For transformational teachers, the goals are academic, social, and spiritual. Annual standardized exams do not measure social and spiritual goals which are immeasurably important for transformational learning. It is vital to have rigorous academic goals and testing, but it is wrong to allow a standardized academic culture to crowd out instruction aimed at the heart. Social goals have to do with relationships with others, like cooperation, tolerance, and empathy. Spiritual goals are similar but emphasize humans as individuals in their hopes, compassion, and dignity. The separation of spiritual from social in this age of digital and tribal influences is needed to bolster individual identity. Cyber bullies as we know can create a social media morality that is vigilante-like in its condemnation of transcendent norms. Students need us teachers to give them learning opportunities that lead toward both the measurable and the immeasurable. Social goals involve social awareness while spiritual goals focus on a self-awareness and personal growth for goodness' sake.

> **Perspective: The Fog of Confusion**
>
> Education can be like a foggy summer morning as the day awaits the hot sun for clarity and definition. What we see early on is not the reality later. Learning is very complex, as complex as human beings, not the simple conception we sometimes think we see, or take for granted. Michael Tomasello

> (2019), a groundbreaking biopsychologist/ontogenist in the tradition of Lev Vygotsky, reminds us that we are uniquely human because we seek emotional attunement with other humans, literally cultivating social intelligence. Our students should have a "shared intentionality" in coordinating and cooperating with others as they develop. Do our schools currently foster these uniquely human intelligences? Perhaps one of U.S. history's best examples of cultivating social intelligence was the relationship between Abraham Lincoln and Frederick Douglas, former slave and brilliantly self-educated (not unlike Lincoln in terms of education). Douglas had no warm feelings for Lincoln two years into the Civil War. Then they met in Lincoln's office. Douglas was inspired with the setting but confronted the president over unfair treatment of Black soldiers. Lincoln listened. Douglas counseled Lincoln on the Emancipation Proclamation. Lincoln listened. After reelection Lincoln delivered his famous Second Inaugural Address, "With malice toward none, with charity for all . . ." in March 1865, one month before his assassination. Douglas was there. Lincoln specifically sought out Douglas for his opinion. Douglas said, "Mr. Lincoln, that was a sacred effort."

Our classrooms often do not cultivate. Many schools for the past two decades have marched to a standardized drumbeat, valuing only the academic goal structures that they think will lead to higher achievement, virtually ignoring social goals and the more individually human spiritual goals. One school leader describes it like this:

> A teacher can teach a child how to be a better person, improve a student in every area socially, improve the study skills of a student, or practically save the life of a student with social-emotional intervention. None of those things seem to matter in this age. That teacher will still be subject to criticism, failure to receive raises, and insecure job stability, if a teacher does not improve on test scores. It is my belief that these are symptoms and failings of this standardized age.

For most of us, we realize that we are spiritual, not material beings in our essence. That ability to seek "emotional attunement" with other human beings speaks to the soul, to a light that should be brightened, not dimmed with worksheets and pacing guides from a lock-step system of drudgery. This sentiment of course is not new. Shakespeare in "As You Like It," said to consider, "Then the whining schoolboy, with his satchel and shining morning face, creeping like a snail, unwilling to school."

Undoubtably, the easiest decisions we make are when we feel we have no other option. To transform learners in a classroom we must be strong and treat our teaching like we have no other choice: Informing lives academically is just not enough. It never has been. We teach for learners, not only to meet their academic needs but to transform their lives.

Effects of Test-Driven Schooling on Students

First, there is the social and emotional damage. As reported by Armstrong (2019) prior to the COVID-19 pandemic, primary-age children increasingly reported migraines and ulcers connected to school performance pressure (Abeles, 2016). One-third of adolescents felt depressed or overwhelmed from school stress (American Psychological Association, 2014). The mental health of current college-age students has declined precipitously, especially white females (Joseph, 2019).

> **Perspective: SEL Efforts**
>
> Educators are now prolifically writing about promoting social and emotional learning (SEL) and supporting students who are evidencing stress and trauma. Dissatisfaction is so great that we are now searching for educational answers. After nearly a century of "back to basics" in the United States, it seems we may be focusing our educational expertise on another basic: mental health in our K–12 schools. SEL is our educators' code for attending to the whole child, which has been a rallying cry for decades.

To hardly anyone's surprise, COVID-19 exacerbated emotional and mental distress among adolescents in particular. According to the Centers for Disease Control (CDC, 2025), 40% of U.S. high school students in 2023 reported persistent feelings of sadness or hopelessness, with 20% considering suicide. More than half of U.S. adolescents reported seeing a mental health care professional in 2023. Undoubtably, COVID-19 played a role as circumstances of isolation and forced distance learning decreased opportunities for social-emotional wellness. We all have a role to play at home and at school in the social and emotional health of our children. At home and at school, the CDC frequently cites "adverse childhood experiences" and "positive childhood experiences" (PCEs) as having significant impact on our students' mental, social, and physical health. The more PCEs the less likely students are to have diagnosed mental health conditions. How can we promote more holistic learning in our roles as teachers? The relater role is all about relationships and should synergize with our work as scholars and practitioners. Building relationships in classrooms is related to freedom to teach.

One of the biggest reasons we choose teaching as our craft and vocation is for "creative license." Teachers want to feel free to teach students within a supportive system of high expectations, but such freedom is now severely limited in many systems and schools. The concept of more teacher autonomy, of "freedom to teach" is resonating in educational communities. Students for their part have had to accept what is taught and the way it is taught; after all they are the primary victims of systems and schools that do not support holistic learning.

It seems clear that educational accountability measures starting in 2001 with NCLB, then Race to the Top-2009, and currently ESSA (Every Student Succeeding Act in 2016) have produced dismal results in educational achievement. In fourth and eighth grades, 60%–67% of our students are still not proficient in reading and mathematics average scores (NAEP, April 10, 2017 Report). The headline is that "national test scores reveal a decade of educational stagnation" in the United States (Barshay, 2018, p. 1). No significant change has occurred since 2015, including among selected racial/ethnic groups. It is noteworthy that this period coincides with the implementation of Common Core Standards or their facsimile in most states. (It is not the Standards per se; it is how teachers are required to teach to them.) The detail is that there has been a decrease in average mathematics scores "for lower performing fourth grade students" and an increase "for higher performing students" (but still below proficiency) since 2015.

In a 2023 update, the National Center for Educational Statistics, which is the primary statistical agency of the fledgling U.S. Department of Education, reported that in the last dozen years (2012–2023) reading scores have declined 7% and math scores have plummeted 14%. Is it not obvious by now, as many have said, that standardized education is a failing solution?

It is very interesting (and surprising to many who think we should test anything that moves) that the United States is far from the most test-crazy country in the world. Most of the top achieving countries give more tests than the United States. The disconnecting problem is that most U.S. teachers are forced to teach to the ones we have. Could it be that the difference is not the tests, but that we are increasingly teaching to them? Can't we do better, especially in allowing more, much more teacher autonomy?

Teacher-Reaction to Challenging Times

When teachers in the trenches read these reports, it is with a sigh. Most teachers want to teach to the whole child, to inspire learners to master what is being studied, and to fulfill every role needed to achieve great results. Jessica, a school leader, laments,

> So often, teachers become overwhelmed by the sheer number of content standards they must teach and the fact that they are held accountable for teaching them all to mastery. Not only does this frustrate teachers, it leaves students in a tailspin trying to learn a little bit about a lot.

Jessica would agree that standardized schools capitalize the "R" in routine as it affects each workday:

> It is so easy to lose focus. A teacher's day is full of so many tasks: Monitor student arrival, take attendance, collect lunch money, lesson plan, reply to texts and emails, make parent phone calls, collect homework, manage student behavior and/or discipline students for poor choices, teach, assess, report the data, teach, assess, report the data, teach, assess… etc. And so goes the life of a teacher.

Schooling has to be more of a preparation for life to its fullest. Life has more meaning if we live it to our potential.

> **Perspective: Freedom as a "Tested-Teacher"**
>
> Great teachers assist students in living to their potential. Freedom to teach to that potential can be found in windows that are still open within the system. High school mathematics teacher Kristin says,
>
> > I have been a 'tested teacher' for many years and there is so much emphasis on standardized testing that I feel people forget to look at our students as whole humans rather than a test score. I will continue to teach the whole child and work on becoming a better transformational teacher.
>
> Freedom is not an answer but a question. How can we manage to keep our calling intact even when "tested?"

Instruction should affect testing. Instead now, what is tested drives instruction. The tail wags the dog. Unfortunately, policy has created school settings where tests and standards are both misused, and this clearly influences the ability of our teachers to construct the combination of caring, challenging, and creative learning environments. Evidence-based teaching methods are required—a good thing. But the skeletal structure of standardized exams—what many educators loathe—is unchanged in the Every Student Succeeding Act (ESSA). All states are required to give annual tests in reading and math in grades 3–8 and once in high school. Testing in science at least three times before graduation is also required. States can develop their own annual achievement tests but 95% of students must be tested. Most states give yearly math and English/language arts tests to all students in grades 3–8 and high school. No reductions or sampling approaches have been allowed.

So what is wrong with making our schools and teachers more accountable for improving student achievement? On the surface, very little. We want to be inclusive so that *all* of our students can learn and even to be models of achievement for the world. Assessment is part of the loop of instructional effectiveness. By definition it is visible feedback about teacher impact (Hattie, 2009). We must evaluate. If we dig below the surface, however, we quickly realize that while we were otherwise occupied with standardizing our schools, we are losing what we were trying to save: our learners.

Perspective: Eval-YOU-ate

Danielle, an urban school supervisor, tells of a parent she briefly overheard in the hallway of a school. She heard the mother yell at the principal, "Testing is not for the kids; it's for you all!" The word "evaluate" has better meaning than "assess" for this writer because a teacher once pointed out it has "u" (you) in it. Current annual assessments for public schools lack the "you," too. When most parents and communities begin to stand up and realize what is obvious to most educators, that the 3-R's now only exist as part of the 4-t's (teaching to the test), and that their children as per policy are often not respected as learners, perhaps change toward more student-centered teaching will occur. Student-centered teaching? The irony is that that was one of our schooling "problems" before the passage of NCLB in 2001.

Solutions

An obvious "solution" is to use data from the myriad of evaluation tools employed across the United States to actually impact individual learning. Cariss and Sullivan (2019) in Chico, CA, have sought to unify a response district-wide for testing data to impact and improve student learning:

> Since embarking on this initiative, we've seen a drastic shift in our schools. Students are being met at their level. We're not forcing the same curriculum on students, ignoring ability level or background. Instead, we're able to offer an individualized experience for each child, where teachers can step in as needed, and parental guardians are always aware of how their student is doing. Initially, our district was concerned that parents would be overwhelmed. But, data is playing a new role in how we're able to interact with parents. Conferences are now a place for deeper insight, and parents can see where their student compares, as well as achievements.

Data can and should be used proactively to support students, and reactively to identify and address district lapses. We see data as a positive tool and something that is perpetually being refined and revised to suit district needs.

(p. 1)

What can we do in our current culture of education that will change it for the better? One thing is to understand that process in education is vital; all of us: Elementary, middle, secondary, even higher education, can commit to a more student-centered ethic. Why is learner-centered pedagogy more about process? Process-oriented teachers are more formative than summative in how they approach their craft. And, when we prioritize formation over summation, we begin to look at our learners differently. We begin to understand the role of trial and error in learning.

Perspective: The Role of "Failure"

Before Elon Musk with Space X was able to "catch" a returning upright rocket on a platform at sea, he and his team experienced many failures. Thomas Edison invented the telegraph, universal stock ticker, phonograph, incandescent light bulb, alkaline battery, and kinetograph (precursor to the motion picture camera). He is often credited for boosting and building the U.S. economy during the Industrial Revolution. Edison once was asked if he ever had failed. "I have not failed. I've just found 10,000 ways that won't work," he replied. "Many of life's failures are people who did not realize how close they were to success when they gave up." George Washington Carver never gave up. His discoveries shared at least two commonalties. They were service-oriented and they were incredibly numerous: adhesives, bleach, chili sauce, instant coffee, shaving cream, linoleum, Worcestershire sauce, and more. He found more than 300 uses for peanuts as well as many derivatives of soybeans, pecans, and sweet potatoes. His career embodied the essence of trial-and-error experimentation as he sought to holistically serve agriculture and human needs.

There is another casualty of high-stakes test obsession: The role of "failure" itself. Some teachers are rather justifiably so concerned about the year-end exam that they do not allow time for failure to succeed! We all know that trial-and-error learning is a rather everlasting process. Perhaps this is because our brain learns effectively through emotion, in this case the emotion of fear from temporary failure. To set up a system of standardized education that systemically discourages trial-and-error pedagogy and learning is not only wrong but tragic.

The goal reset needs to change from achievement testing to transforming learners academically, socially, and spiritually. Even within the current testing structure, in the "meantime," we educators can begin to reimagine pedagogy as reconnecting learning to the learner. Education is for our children not the test-makers.

Final Thoughts

The role of testing has been seriously and even tragically misconstrued over the first three decades of the 21st century. Of course exams can hold learners accountable and provide indicative results for schools. Tests have multiple purposes, but informing teachers of their impact on students is the most important one if we desire transformational learning. What learners demonstrate on an exam should provide useful individual feedback to assist teachers with their goals and strategies. John Hattie's (2015) "visible learning" means we cannot transform students unless their learning is visible to us in some way. The Chico, CA, example, where testing is wholly used for improving student learning, is meaningfully instructive. It conforms to basic pedagogical principles, which in this age is ironically nonconforming.

Knowing our learners in a diagnostic sense can be aided by authentic learning where students can apply new knowledge in different contexts. The psychological term *transfer* means we can show our learning in different places. Some factors that affect it are authentic learning, teaching principles rather than facts, and lots of examples and practice.

Tests cannot measure everything and we must not let the measurable crowd out the immeasurable in social and spiritual goals. Schools must identify with shared intentionality uniquely human intelligences, like "emotional attunement" with other human beings.

Test-driven schooling is increasingly affecting (or infecting) students with social and emotional damage. It also is affecting educators who are demoralized and dropping out of education as a profession. The lack of freedom to teach in creative and autonomous ways, like more usage of trial-and-error learning, is demoralizing many teachers.

Standardized schooling says what is tested affects instruction, just the opposite of best practice which says that what is taught should affect testing. Standardization influences the ability of teachers to construct the combination of caring and challenging classroom environments that foster transformational learning.

6

Challenging Learners and Building Hope

Myth # 6	Fact # 6
The best teachers are those with a reputation for being hard.	Rigor is not productive when it means excessive and irrelevant requirements for learners. Rigor is good when it challenges students to their maximum potential. Learners need that hope.

What is the greatest challenge for a transformational teacher? Many might say it is putting together the three roles of scholar, practitioner, and relater in synergy. Some would say it is learning to teach beyond the test. For some it is learning to be our authentic selves in the classroom, real people with real emotion. For some it is not teaching the same lesson twice—realizing that every class of individuals is different with different needs. For some it is allowing students the freedom to learn how to learn. For some it is reconciling their creative calling with the expectation of teaching standard by standard. For some teachers it is the challenge of translating and conveying our love of subject to novice learners. And, for other teachers it is confronting the humbling fact that teaching can occur without learning, despite how passionate we are about knowledge and subject.

Regardless of what challenges us the most as teachers, good teachers have always found a way to translate their love of knowledge and subject to learners. Rigor is a teacher's desire for students to join the great world of knowledge. Rigorous teaching is a combination of high expectations, expertise, and clear communication. It all begins with teachers continuously falling in love with their subject. It is passion and enthusiasm, but not the unbridled kind that loses touch with students' needs. Scholarly teachers are accomplished professionals and ought to be celebrated.

Perspective: To Be or Not to Be

Educated that is. Terri, an elementary school teacher, thinks that people really do not value being educated anymore. A number of people share this sentiment because of the standardized sameness of many of our contemporary schools. It is also true that this is not a new feeling among educators of past generations. Whatever the era of schooling, elements of proper challenge must be present (with some sprinkles of novelty). And, students must enter our classrooms with hope kindled by sensitive teachers.

K–12 teachers suffer an unfair apples-to-oranges comparison with higher education in terms of scholarly work. Instead, we must clarify our definition to say that teacher-scholars are those who have reason to be superbly confident in their subject. Thankfully, social media, podcasts, and blogging outlets more often allow K–12 teacher-scholars to be recognized for their expertise. The most reasonable outlet for scholarly expression of K–12 teachers (besides good teaching itself) is speaking, not writing. The scholar role in the Transformational Pedagogy Model is just one of three, with teacher-practitioner and teacher-relater serving as demanding roles, too. Perhaps this combination demonstrates how uncommon it is for teachers to fulfill all three roles of transformational teaching, primarily because of work expectations for U.S. teachers. Educators keen to their craft work harder, enduring more stress than most any profession. The incentive for role-holism in education centers on inspiring learning through knowing, doing, and caring.

Rigor occurs in productive and unproductive forms in our classrooms. We all have stories to tell about "rigorous" teachers. In high school, I had an algebra teacher who would throw erasers out of frustration at boys (never girls) who were just not keeping up with him. His reputation was of a volatile, rigorous teacher because he was emotional and somewhat a scholar in his subject. The obvious truth was that he had no interest in attuning his subject to the learning needs of all his students.

Perspective: The Challenge of Solving a Problem

I also had a graduate studies professor who opened a new world of inquiry teaching for me. He was well-read and articulate and creative. He also knew my name even though the class was large. One day he presented a series of map overlays of an unknown country with the question, "If you were a settler, where on this map is best to locate a city?" He placed one transparent overlay at a time on a projection, each containing more geographic and climate information. After a time I happened to recognize that it was an upside down version of Australia. He saw me after class and congratulated me (note that his praise was privately given, which research shows is much more effective). This teacher sought to challenge his students with a mystery island exercise in guided inquiry. His students could use their current knowledge to analyze and then synthesize a problem posed as a question. I still remember the class because the teacher taught in a way with which I was unfamiliar and connected a sense of agency to me.

And, there was a literature teacher who was brilliant with her subject and determined that her students upload her brilliance. Each week we wrote a paper using a bibliography that she provided. The course was so overwhelming that her students could not muster interest after a couple weeks. The teacher was befuddled that we were not learning but never asked the learners why. She simply pressed on. It was one of the most difficult classes I have experienced because the challenge eventually became frustration and the subject (literature) became irrelevant to her students.

Hope in the Classroom

We have a crisis of despair in contemporary U.S. public schools. The burden on educators is heavy. Even in crisis, there is reason for hope within the system because teachers know they are there for the students. The research is strong, very strong on the effect that hopeful teachers can have on students' ability to succeed. Hope is a feeling but it is more because it can translate into an enthusiasm that impacts student learning. It involves expectations for and belief in good things happening. Hope and success are inextricably related for both teachers and learners!

Snyder (1995) calls hope a belief consisting of both agency (a "will") and pathways (a "way"). In other words, learners who have hope carry a perspective of persistence and productivity. To state it bluntly, some discouraged learners may say, "No way." All teachers must say, "Yes way." To achieve success, learners must have the ability to perform independently of their teachers. Students can be encouraged to believe in themselves and their ability to learn and perform. Sometimes teachers can inspire through creativity even as they challenge learners with skill lessons.

Creatively Teaching Grammar

Cottingham (2024) writes about integrating grammar skills in creative writing by having students practice writing dialogue in short stories. The practice assists in placing punctuation with quotation marks while also working on verb tense and subject-verb agreement. She also suggests "missing-words stories" where students create stories but omit words like adjectives, adverbs, or specific tense requirements. Peers must try to fill in the blanks, making for rigorous interaction. Something hard (or at least tedious—grammar) can be softened with creative thinking by teachers. It is teaching with the hope of really believing in the potential of every student, and communicating that belief to the learner. Such teachers are seeking to fulfill all three roles of transformational teaching.

In this mix of challenge and creativity is a specific expectation for positive outcomes. U.S. schools vary greatly of course, but many teachers experience a certain despair in not feeling free to teach the way they desire. And, many students are disaffected. Despair is the opposite of hope and in brain-science is related to fear, which is a heavily studied wired emotion in our brains.

To paraphrase a line from an old movie, transformational teachers must remember that when we find disaffected and disadvantaged learners in our classrooms, *those are their circumstances not the learners themselves*. Hope can counter despair.

Jensen (2005) describes the impact of negative emotions and over-stress on brain function, specifically involving heightened cortisol levels. This secretion of the brain-hormone cortisol in times of negative emotions (which is actually a good thing in "fight-or-flight" situations) is a fact, and at least in part explains why we tend to remember negative experiences more than positive ones (Abercrombie et al., 2003; Ito et al., 2001). Cortisol is known to impact multiple cognitive domains including attention, perception, memory, and emotional processing.

This hormone in prolonged amounts (Posey, 2019) "can actually become toxic to the hippocampus, the region of the brain fundamental to learning" (p. 15). Remember it is the hippocampus that allows us to sort out and remember who and what we know and don't know. Interestingly in talking about "plasticity," Posey (2019) and Jensen (2005) claim both sensory experience (outside) and even our thoughts (inside) can change our brains.

Perspective: Getting Along with Ourselves

Someone, originally not sure who, said, "Hope is not a plan." While most of us cannot argue with that observation—hope is a feeling or a belief—I suspect we can agree that the best plans are laid on a foundation of hope. If we are hopeful long enough, it can become a life skill. Overdoses of stress seem a reality for many teachers, which lead to a lot of bad things: irritability, mood swings, compulsiveness, depression, to name a few. But even in the worst of times we can find ourselves by investing in others, like our students. Naming it (overstress) is different from blaming it, and is more therapeutic. Giving our students choices and asking the "worth knowing" questions of our curriculum can help us get along with ourselves.

Perhaps many of us have had the experience of waking up one day, maybe it's during a vacation, or a long, boring drive, or after a stressful day with students, where we realize that we need to change our behavior, or maybe even alter or change the environment. The realization is likely based on the hope that we can do better if we begin to think and feel differently about our lives. The epiphany is probably born out of a long set of experiences over time. Good mental health is to confront ourselves with reality checks as often as we can. And, our brains are wired for the emotions to follow through on our new priorities.

Perspective: The Brain's Reward System

Positive emotions are more complex in the brain but also receive priority for memory (Jensen, 2005). "Dopamine is a neurotransmitter that is linked to pleasure and our perception of positive experiences" (p. 57). Schultz (2000) reports that this neurotransmitter is a part of our brain's reward system, controlling our ability to predict and enjoy pleasurable experiences. For example, eating our favorite dessert or, seemingly paradoxically, indulging in exercise releases dopamine. Even positive smells can work to release dopamine. Real estate agents seem to have known this for a long time, encouraging sellers to bake bread or cookies before an open house! Locklear (2025) reports that studies show even infants (age four months to two years) have positive memories, showing a "lit-up hippocampus" and smile.

Teachers need the pleasure that comes from the positive experience of changing lives. We often do not receive the positive feedback we crave as professionals, at least not in a timely way. But we can change the learning environment so that our students can delight in learning. Their dopamines can help make them and their teachers full of hope. This is the stuff of mutual transformation.

A caveat here is that the same neurotransmitter is released in boys and girls playing videogames, explaining why (1) the experience is addictive, and (2) it is so difficult for parents to pry their children away from playing. This brain-science explains why life is replete with examples of youth and adults whose positive traits or strengths can become weaknesses if not monitored or disciplined.

Hope and Challenge

Engaging learners is a relatively complex combination of what is outside the learner (meaningful curriculum, teacher pedagogy, and support) and what is inside (developmental readiness and emotional connection in the brain). As teachers we give most of our attention to the external factors, to what we experience with our five senses. External factors are vital. For example, research suggests that the presence of Black male teachers is significantly important to the success of Black students. Studies linked to the National Bureau of Economic Research (Gershenson et al., 2021) found that Black students who had at least one Black male teacher in elementary school were 39% less likely to drop out of high school and 13% more likely to enroll in college (and 32% more likely with two Black male teachers). Currently, only 2% of U.S. public school teachers are Black males. Role models are an essential part of inspiring hope.

To engage we need ways to reach what is internal and invisible as well as the external and sensory. If our ultimate goal is transformation, to encourage and support students reaching their individual potential, we are more likely to create the mix of external and internal factors needed for an engaged learning environment.

Finding Hope

In a 2017 film, *Darkest Hour*, the wife of Winston Churchill, Clementine, counseled him in one of his lowest moments: "You are strong because you are imperfect; you are wise because you have doubts." She was trying to give him hope even as Churchill in 1940 had the weight of the world, literally, on his shoulders as Nazi Germany was conquering all of Europe and threatening Britain. This was a spiritual moment where he despaired for support from within his own government in order to fight the enemy without. He had a self-awareness of how to lead and what to do, but he at that moment needed encouragement and confidence to free him to act. Teachers need hope in order to inspire such resilience.

The academic goal for every teacher at any level should be to inspire and create learners who can function with some freedom and independence. The social and spiritual goals for teachers involve modeling kindness, compassion, and wisdom. We can "create" self-directed learners who are empowered to be more curious about themselves as well as to question the information they receive. The hope is that we all as educators can patiently learn to somehow stand outside ourselves as we look at classrooms and life itself.

Perspective: Making the Invisible Visible

Allison Posey (2019) in her writings about engaging the brain, makes the point that at times it can be impossible to know that someone is engaged, what someone is thinking and feeling. She uses the example of her own children walking under and through Niagara Falls Cave of the Winds. Her daughter was an easy read, stretching out her arms and screaming with laughter. Her son was not so expressive, instead staying inside his comfort zone. It turned out that "both kids loved the experience and described it as their favorite part of the vacation" (p. 126). Engagement for students is spontaneous, even when they may not show it, with effects that are lasting. Transformation occurs when teachers create a learning environment where challenging but hopeful connections can occur.

Bruning et al. (2011) cite a number of studies that reveal significant relationships between both teachers' and learners' expressed hope and academic achievement. Research from Babyak et al. (1993), Snyder (1995), and Snyder et al. (2002) confirm the relationship between hope and higher academic outcomes. Yoshinobu (1989) found that people with high hope demonstrated significantly more self-determination in the face of failure. Lopes and Cunha (2008) used Snyder's hope-inventory (with questions like "My past experiences have prepared me well for the future," and "There are lots of ways around any problem.") and determined that people scoring high were likely to be more goal-oriented in several domains, including academics, job, personal relationships, health, and spiritual development. Peterson and Byron (2008) found higher-hope individuals solve problems more effectively and are rated higher in their job performance.

The Peterson and Byron research confirms what we see in our academic workplaces. High hopes inspire problem-solving and high performance. High morale is directly related to our hopes for success. Low morale often comes when people do not feel like they are a part of a team. This fact would speak to leadership in our schools, but part of this leadership, a huge part, is government decision-makers. Teachers (the best are leaders themselves) and school leaders are duty-bound and seek to follow the "rules" set from above. Within those rules, why not some "subversive activity" like creating a more student-centered learning environment?

Standardization imposed top-down is an enemy of creativity in education but is not the only enemy. We as educators who are not inspired to try new and nontraditional ways of transforming learning are also obstacles. Great teachers are great leaders with inspiration to encourage learning.

Perspective: Teachers Can Be Inspiring Leaders

Jim Collins in *Good to Great* (2001) carefully outlines his observations related to great leaders, what he called "Level 5" leaders. He says such leaders have two sides: professional will and personal humility. He suggests that *will*-leaders need to look "in the mirror, not out the window, to apportion responsibility for poor results, never blaming other people, external factors, or bad luck;" and that *humble*-leaders should look "out the window, not in the mirror, to apportion credit for the success of the company—to other people, external factors, and good luck" (p. 36). Such driven, non-egocentric leaders encourage others, whether teacher to student, or school leader to teacher, to participate in the process of engaging learning, that is, allowing teachers-leaders the autonomy to create their own learning environments and pedagogies. Then they have the ownership, the agency needed for high hopes. Communication is basic for leaders to create high morale: Not just communication when things are going badly, but especially when things are in process or going well.

Bruning et al. (2011) summarize, saying that (1) scores on the hope inventory seem to be independent of intellectual ability; (2) scores are unrelated to gender; and (3) some people may be predisposed to be more hopeful than others. It seems apparent from "hope" research as well as other social cognitive research, that teachers and the learning environment they create are key to students' expecting and realizing success. Lynsey, an elementary teacher, reflects:

> We must teach in a way that is counter to the culture. Focusing on academics exclusively does not produce the well-rounded citizens that we need to ensure a bright future. Teachers must teach in such a way that inspires students to learn more in depth, inspires them to be a better persons with values, and inspires them to find purpose in their lives.

Michael Tomasello (2019) says that the process of learners' internalizing knowledge and belief is "nothing other than role-reversal imitation used in a flexible way: The child imitates others directing her behavior or, alternately, imitates herself teaching others, with herself substituted as learner" (p. 153). Teachers must ask themselves continually, "What am I modeling that is worthy of imitation?" This work coincides with Vygotsky's emphasis on significant others, adults and peers, assisting learners in internalization. Obviously self-belief is a learned behavior! And, it is vital to successful performance.

Creating Challenge

Challenge with teachers can be tricky. With higher standards we somehow assume transfer of learning if difficult material is taught. Further irony is that the federal mandates of the last two decades contain elements intended to boost student achievement with the hope of increased productivity in the United States. But none of the elements has increased student engagement in learning or test scores. Schmoker (2018) says that "these standards . . . were bound to become a default guide to instruction" (p. 34). Teachers like a recipe for instruction—usually we like it too much because we yearn to make the complicated simple. Teaching standard by standard is a bad recipe.

Schmoker argues for prioritizing the simplicity and clarity of proven methods. Across the curriculum, he makes the case for deep reading, effective writing, discussion, and speaking. As he concludes, "Reading and writing are central to good schooling—and they influence each other reciprocally. Writing reveals how much and how well we read—even as it makes us better readers and thinkers" (p. 41).

Perspective: The Challenge and Reward of Writing

Learning always seems to follow when we meet a challenge, and writing down our thoughts with regularity is often quite a challenge in itself. Good teachers have long encouraged their students to keep journals, even though the experience can be difficult. It is like the self-discipline of doing something we don't want to do every day. Primary teachers successfully use language experience to teach reading, recording five or six year old's thoughts, transcribing them, then asking the semi-amazed readers to "read" their own words. Teachers who write blogs, articles, and books discover that they enhance their vocabulary, improve their speaking skills, and transform their teaching through more self-confidence. Composing our own words is a challenge but can be immensely rewarding.

Indeed, there is something comprehensive about writing as one of the skills of literacy with reading, listening, and speaking. Reading and listening are receptive skills and are the hallmark of educated people. If we want to be a good student, we read! If we want to be a good leader, we listen!

Speaking and writing are expressive skills. Learn to speak well and people will listen! Learn to write well and a satisfying life will follow! Writing frees more productive speaking. Good writing forces us to express our thoughts with more clarity and precision than extemporary speaking. While a focused discussion remains an irreplaceable learning mode because of its power to socialize and to stimulate critical thinking, writing has the most potential to educate. And, when we add the critical element of timely constructive feedback from a teacher who carries a transformational attitude, the learner becomes totally engaged in the curriculum.

Final Thoughts

When we describe a teacher as demanding, we generally mean that the expectations are so high that they seem unreasonable. All of us have had teachers like this; usually these teachers know their subject and expect their students to follow suit. The "unreasonable" part is crucial of course. If the demands are excessive or irrelevant to the point of producing frustration, learning is not produced. Worse yet, the aftereffects of the frustration can linger with learners (brain-experts would say excessive toxic hormonal cortisol is released in the body), affecting confidence and blocking learning.

Thus, in this context, challenge and hope become significant factors, even flashpoints, especially in standardized schools where teacher sensitivity is not as big of an expectation as "rigor." It is instructive to discuss and compare the scholar-role for public school teachers to that of teachers in higher education. It is an unfair, even to the point of irrelevance, comparison because busy schoolteachers have less time to nurture and build their scholarship. A salient point is that teachers can construct a stronger scholar role with speaking more than writing because of the time constraints, but teachers still should be encouraged to write whenever possible.

For optimal learning, for transformational learning, students need the challenge of developmentally appropriate subject matter and expectations. With today's core standards and test-driven schools, appropriate challenge is almost certainly a "challenge" within a challenge. Sensitive teachers are needed to perceive the difference between a challenge and a frustration for learners. Here is where hope is crucial. Students must feel hopeful that they can succeed. So do teachers.

Studies reveal that there is a significant relationship between both teachers' and learners' expressed hopes and the academic achievement of students. Indeed higher-hope individuals solve problems more effectively and are rated higher in job performance. Leadership can encourage teachers to seek classroom autonomy, to own the process of engaging students, thus creating hope for teachers and students alike.

I have documented the tremendous morale issues created by standardized education for teachers and students alike, resulting in teacher flight from the profession and student emotional issues. Finding a balance of challenge and hope in our public school classrooms seems one of the most significant issues of contemporary U.S. schooling.

7

Finding Joy in Learning

Myth # 7	Fact # 7
Teachers with a reputation for making learning "fun" have sacrificed rigorous standards.	The best teachers connect to emotion as a basic human structure, finding ways to incorporate joy in learning.

Joy is one of the wired emotions in our brains along with anger, sorrow, and fear (some neurologists add surprise and disgust). Why not seek joy as we teach and learn? Paradoxically, in learning we often find joy in the midst of fear. With the right "dosage" of challenge, fear is engendered—a good thing, because fear of failure is a huge motivator.

Perspective: The Flight of the Bumblebee

Joy can happen along the way! Learning sometimes is more intense, even painful, but most of us want more than intensity and pain out of life. When we couple challenging instruction with inspirational tags, "fun facts," we direct learners' attention and concentration. For example, learning about pollination is interesting and one of the best pollinators is the bumblebee, which with its aircraft-carrier body has to beat its relatively tiny wings 200 times/second to stay aloft. Inspiration must come before information. Where does the power of joy come from? It comes from within. There is no need to sacrifice standards as we seek to motivate our students. And, there is no need not to seek joyful classroom experiences as part of a balanced goal set.

Benjamin Bloom got it right as he and his associates placed thinking (cognitive), feeling (affective), and doing (psychomotor) into taxonomies. Most scholars early on emphasized the cognitive domain, but brain science has highlighted the affective, social-emotional realm as a key to learning. Krathwohl et al. (1964) with their "Affective Domain" focused on the subjective to provide context and relevance needed for learning. Our feelings, values, appreciations, enthusiasms, motivations, and attitudes are addressed in this domain in a hierarchical manner. They explain that a process of internalization takes us as learners from a general awareness level to an affective point of behavioral internalization and commitment. Narrowing the curriculum and the classroom environment to pedantic academics is needless and harmful. We perhaps know joy best when we miss it our lives.

Perspective: Remember Play?

Saying it bluntly, many U.S. schools are killjoys. We have even moved onto the sacred ground of five-year-olds with increased academics. Froebel invented the kindergarten over two centuries ago to systematize play for young children. He organized it around "gifts and occupations" because he knew that children needed a structure to launch their creative impulses into joyful experiences. It freed them to play. All of us in life have been surprised by joy while we were focusing on something else. Distracted teenagers need play, too. The COVID-19 pandemic was especially hard on teens who were cut off from whatever in-person relationships they still had in this age of social media loneliness. One solution for teenage play: get them outside! Find a good shade tree and hold a class.

Howard Gardner's theory of "multiple intelligences" (1999) is a refreshing reminder that learners are more than an IQ score. (To continue to stress IQ in education might rank as another myth on our list.) Students are an amalgam of intelligences, of talents or strengths that uniquely define them. If we had to choose, and we do not have to choose, his theory is more valuable in teaching us how to perceive students than how to teach to each of the intelligences. We do great harm when we do not celebrate the talents of individual learners, and not teach to them in a mindful way. And, part of this celebration is addressing the holism of bringing joy to the school environment.

Joy matters in schooling. Neuroscientist Amy Takabori (2020) says that our brains release hormonal dopamine (and other neural transmitters) when we experience joy, referring to it as a "save button" because its presence promotes development of long-term memory. Thus, joy is an emotion, but it is also a disposition or affective goal that we can nurture in ourselves and our students.

Spiritual Goals

A key area of the holistic model for transformational pedagogy is the realm of spiritual goals. When we invite joy into our classrooms (Kessler, 2000), we are seeking to connect to an inner life, what poets have called a spark of light and wonder. This invisible spirit is something we all know is there because, among other reasons, as humans we have a unique ability to think about our thoughts. We are able to will ourselves to think about our strengths and weaknesses. From our students' perspective, they long for something beyond the material, beyond the secular experience of sight and sounds, toward a deeper and more sacred awareness. We are metacognitive, but we are also meta-spiritual. We want to understand nature, social justice, questions about creation and evolution, our ancestral lineage. C. S. Lewis said that we are not bodies with souls but souls with bodies attached.

This understanding is why it is so vital that we see our students for who they really are. To say it another way, we teach whole persons who are soul-persons. Why settle for only what we see physically and academically? Rachael Kessler (2000) said that it is not a question of whether we should teach to spiritual transcendence, but how. Students want to find purpose in their lives and teachers, even in the secular realm of public schools, can assist.

Perspective: Soul-Purpose

When we include humor, celebrations, enjoyment of nature, inspirational movies, and, significantly, physical movement in our classrooms, we allow a context for students to exit their self-absorption and for teachers to display genuineness with their learners. Such realness in teachers touches who students are, a very human mix of searching and fear and confusion. Learners who find themselves with transformational teachers ask questions about what they should do in life, about what happens after death, about finding meaning, about why bad things happen, about whether things happen for a reason. These are all soul-purpose questions and are ignored at our students' peril. Public school teachers must avoid the religious in this context but not the spiritual.

Most educators believe that they need to connect to the indestructible essence of students because they themselves have to cope with the same questions. Someone or something larger than they is revealed in the longing to be whole. The Hebrew word, *Shalom*, sums up the peace and wholeness our students are seeking. Joy is always waiting to be revealed because it is locked, or at least restrained, inside us. Its revelation unlocks learning in the brain (Jensen & McConchie, 2020). Connecting the curriculum to the total realm of affective learning does not have to be planned—it can be a matter of recognizing a learning opportunity.

Storm the Hill

An urban school leader, Keisha, accompanied nearly 300 high school students to her state's capitol city for a "Storm the Hill" student day. Students were grouped with legislative representatives when they arrived. Each school was supposed to send ten students but on this day only one was sent from a particular school. Kami was a junior who came dressed in her Sunday best with pearls and handbag to match. All the other students wore "Storm the Hill" t-shirts. She had noticed the young woman at lunch and commented on how lovely she looked. Kami's face lit up with a smile, especially since she obviously knew she was dressed differently than anyone else, and since she knew no one.

During ensuing conversation she told the educator that she wanted to make a good impression on the lawmakers because someday she wanted to be one. Kami said her dad would be so proud to tell her family in Guatemala she was a state senator or House member. In that moment Keisha knew it wasn't about the trip, or schedule, or even the sessions. It was all about a young 11th-grade student named Kami who needed support. The school leader connected with the student. They mutually decided to hang out together as the educator became caught up in Kami's enthusiasm, realizing both were experiencing the heart, mind, and soul of education. Keisha with Kami found herself fulfilling exactly why she entered the profession: She was encouraging the spirit of a motivated learner.

Our school leader and Kami model the joy in learning concept on their field trip. A field trip done right is part of a classroom curriculum. Kami's field trip was productive and successful because it embodied meaningful engagement. It was truly authentic learning.

Authentic Relationships

Inviting joy into the education of our children demands an affective response from educators, whether public or private. Ultimately it is not so much what we do or say, but who we are as teachers. Students gravitate to transformational teachers because they model spiritual and social qualities that transcend the academic. The Ancients spoke of spiritual dispositions that we educators can carry with us, like: Compassion, patience, and persistence in the face of obstacles; optimism of seeing the good in learners; peace in the sense that we believe things will work out; self-control which leads to wisdom and empathy; tolerance in not needing to force our way; kindness; and yes, joy. These are universal traits that students long to see in their teachers. The expectation is that we can aspire to be the whole package of knowers, doers, and inspirers. Of course what we do and say are important as we recognize they are manifestations of who we are. Knowing our students is crucial and is facilitated by teachers who are open and genuine. We can seek ways to know our students.

> **Perspective: Pass the Ball**
>
> Here's a twist on the classroom ritual of having students introduce themselves at the beginning of the year (or the beginning of a course). Find a child's soft rubber ball, maybe softball size, which will provide some psychomotor interaction. Write several topics on the board like: my favorite meal, how we picked a name for our dog/cat, my best vacation ever, my dream car, my favorite movie, favorite song and other such topics. Begin the activity by tossing the ball to a student, with instructions that he/she, after giving his/her name, must choose one of the topics and talk about it for a short period of time (maybe 30 seconds). Then that student passes the ball to another student at random (a toss not a handoff). The next student then follows suit until all students have tossed and caught the ball. This activity is about relationships and fun, about knowing each other. It can be a "big reveal" that solidifies a healthy classroom environment.

Most students will "reveal" themselves in a safe and supportive context. And, teacher-answers to soul-searching questions in a classroom can be diplomatic even as we know students are looking and watching who we are outside of the classroom. They desperately want authority figures who can guide them with compassion and clarity as they form their own identities. Teachers with attitudes of integrity invite joy in the classroom, which is closely linked to creativity. To be creative is to be exuberant about learning.

Unleashing Creativity

The 2022 Program for International Student Assessment (PISA) in its third set of results (Sharp, 2024) measured creativity in 15-year-olds across 64 countries. We know from polls of teachers and their communities that creativity is highly valued but under-encouraged in contemporary, test-driven schools. Interestingly, U.S. schools were not included because of differing instructional practices among states and districts. Singapore, Latvia, South Korea, and Denmark led the world in developing "appropriate and original ideas" (p. 2). Students were asked to react to a comic strip and fill in dialogue, and to give ideas on how to make a crowded library more accessible. Those with a creative growth mindset performed significantly better. Teachers' encouragement made a big difference in "whether students developed original approaches to problems" (p. 3).

The Organization for Economic Cooperation and Development (OECD) operates PISA and recommends several teaching practices that support creativity, such as novel and challenging curriculum, skill in at least one academic domain, development of learning products, open inquiry on problem solving, time for student reflection and feedback. Interestingly, "girls performed better in all areas of creative thinking than boys did" (p. 5). The areas tested were scientific problem solving, social problem solving, written expression, and visual expression.

The latest PISA results are quite compelling to me for a couple reasons. For the first time these international researchers attempted to capture measurements on creativity, surely a welcome undertaking. Singapore, a small city-state in Asia, led the way in math, reading, and science achievement, but also in creative expressions. This is a country that for nearly two decades has pursued the goal of going beyond its test meritocracy to a talent meritocracy like the United States (Zacharia, 2006), desiring to imitate the United States in creativity, adventure, and challenging conventional wisdom. One irony is that the United States is not even included in the testing for creativity. Apparently teaching practices were so different across states that researchers could not review them and include them.

Another finding of interest is the gender differences on creativity measures favoring girls. It is a testament perhaps to changing role modeling, but a caveat for this research is that the study is done with one age group of 15-year-old girls and boys. Another compelling finding is that teachers set the tone for creative thinking in their classrooms. The greater the challenge the more the support of teachers led to success. Students need the support of teachers in fostering creativity. When teachers set a creative tone, the research shows their students are 27% more likely to find success in solving scientific problems.

Good results demand good process. We must "scrutinize the obvious," as Dallas Willard (1998) has said. How should we teach? As noted earlier, in transformational teaching a mathematical equation applies. Why we teach = Who we teach. Who comes before how. Our rationale, our mission, our purpose, our personal identity, and philosophy in education must center on our students if we desire to adapt the roles and pedagogy and attitudes that great classroom teaching demands.

Affective Process

The process that is teaching begins with a caring knowledge of our students. A veteran teacher shared, "Always teach as if your child is in your classroom." The idea is to share knowledge with our students by connecting to the potential embedded in their lives. Notice: This will be a hard truth for some—it is not about seeing the learning of our subject as the goal of teaching. Our subject matter is a critical piece of schooling, but our knowledge of subject and even our pedagogy become a means to the end of transforming students. The joy of learning is a process.

Perspective: Art and Science=Good Process

Walter Isaacson's biography of Leonardo Da Vinci includes (of course) a full chapter on Da Vinci's masterpiece, the Mona Lisa. The biographer describes the painting as a culmination of a learning process that included scientific and artistic knowledge. So passionate was the artist about this painting that he never sold it, keeping it in Florence, Milan, Rome, and France and improving it until his death. Da Vinci studied human anatomy, optics, and vision to perfect Mona Lisa's famous smile. The anatomist found that the muscle that purses the lips is the same muscle that forms the lower lip. It can pucker on its own without the upper lip. He drew the fine lines of that gentle smile with the ends of the mouth turned down almost imperceptibly. If we stare at the mouth directly, Isaacson notes, she appears not to be smiling. But if we gaze at her eyes and cheeks, the shadows and soft sfumato "make her lips seem to turn upward into a subtle smile. The result is a smile that flickers brighter the less you search for it" (p. 490). And, such was his mastery of light's optical effects, Da Vinci paints the pupil of Mona Lisa's right eye slightly larger because it is the one more directly facing the source of light. Emotion is there: Pleasure causes our eyes to widen, one faster than the other depending on the light. Lisa was pleased to see us!

As noted, Da Vinci never sold his masterpiece, the "Mona Lisa." The reasons are speculative, but that subtle smile stayed with the artist for his lifetime. What came out of a complex, comprehensive, and deeply reflective process was an enduring product that has brought joy to centuries of generations of art lovers.

Learning itself is often tedious, requiring a persistence that depends on strong motivation to be transformational. What stays with us when we learn? It is usually something that is impactful to our life experience, something that is meaningful to us because it touches our emotions. Those emotions are on a short list because our brains, as noted above, are hardwired with them. All of our feelings like happiness, nostalgia, frustration, passion, boredom, and more emanate from these hardwired emotions. Teachers with intentionality can connect with the cerebral foundations of learning.

One of the most powerful sets of research in education involves something that is quite joyful for teachers, parents, and children (of all ages). It is storytelling and more specifically, reading good books to children. Research shows a strong connection to development of vocabulary, improvement of comprehension skills, background knowledge, and emotional intelligence when parents and teachers read books to young children (Debaryshe, 2008; Mol & Bus, 2011; Payne et al., 1994).

Perspective: Three Billy Goats Gruff

It may seem simplistic, but stories like the 19th-century Norwegian folktale, *Three Billy Goats Gruff*, endure for a reason. The reason is it touches our emotions. The heroes of the story are three male goats who need to cross a bridge to access their grazing ground. The goats' problem is that a fearsome troll lives under the bridge who likes to kill and eat anything that attempts to cross it. The three goats come in small, medium, and large sizes, a number and a sequence that is familiar in good stories through the ages. The smallest one goes first and persuades the troll to wait for the medium-sized one because he would make a better meal. The middle Billy goat does the same, appealing to the troll's gluttonous instincts, leading to the largest goat who is more than a match for the hideous troll. He throws him into the deep water with his big horns, effectively drowning the monster and making the bridge a safe crossing to a happy ever after.

A good, old story which now comes with beautifully drawn illustrations brings joy. The goats outsmart the troll, playing on his worse instincts to achieve their goal of crossing to greener pastures. The elements of fear and joy are evident because fear is overcome with wile and courage. Attention is captured and the art of persuasion is highlighted. Transformational learning can be achieved.

A reason we lose the intrinsic joy of learning is the distraction of life itself. For adults we get caught up in work and paying rent and mortgages and parenting. For children, life may be theoretically simpler, but they are not really in control as compared to adults. The institution of schooling itself evolves from more student-centered primary grades to more subject-centered middle and high school grades. A self-contained nurturing teacher becomes a distant memory by the time learners hit fifth grade (or earlier in some schools). And, when we add the stress of their growing awareness of issues at home, the extrinsic pressure of test-driven curriculum and pedagogy, and the technological temptation of addictive cell phones, social media, and video games, our students have sailed into a perfect storm.

How do we promote intrinsic motivation (the phenomenon of eager learners) even as studies show a decrease in a desire to learn from elementary to secondary schools (Lepper et al., 2005; Ormrod, 2012; Wigfield et al., 2006)? Teachers, according to Ormrod, *can*:

- Focus more on authentic learning where they relate topics to students' lives and the everyday world outside the classroom walls. For example, ask, "Your parents always buy a good used car instead of a new one. What are the economics behind that?"
- Model intrinsic learning by teaching students to trust the process of learning. Good test scores and good grades follow from the love of learning. We learn to love learning by participating in learner-centered activities where choices are allowed.
- Build self-efficacy in students by following the "Goldilocks Principle" of not too easy and not too challenging. Easy is boring. Too hard is frustrating. A sensitive, transformational teacher knows the difference and how to monitor students' interaction with subject matter.

- Help students' feeling of ownership in learning. Having ownership is what educational psychologists call self-determination, which is essential for self-autonomy. As an adult, consider the feeling you had when you completely paid off a debt, like a car note, for example. When we own something, it quite simply is ours!
- Provide consistently constructive feedback. It is a teacher's job to provide constructive and detailed feedback. Teachers are in a strategic position via expertise and authority to assist learners with their learning by taking the time to diagnose and correct mistakes. Trial-and-error learning (perhaps the most efficient way to learn) does not occur in classroom environments that are negative and punishing.
- Meet students' nonacademic needs and "students are more likely to focus on their schoolwork." Much of this book centers on that statement. Teachers who desire engaged learning must create an environment that's "orderly and predictable but also psychologically warm and supportive" (p. 458).

Instead of dry, emotionless academics, teachers can invigorate learning with humor and fun. Pedantic academics (need I say it?) is not engaging.

Perspective: Inviting Joy

It is a neurological fact that students will remember more if they have feelings, negative or positive, about their studies. Edison's discovery of the viability of a carbon filament in a vacuum in a lightbulb is exciting learning. Social injustice in American history like the "Trail of Tears" in the 1830s can make us angry. Great poetry and music often convey peace and serenity, even though their authors and composers may have led troubled lives. Robert Frost's poem of "Stopping by the Woods on a Snowy Evening" is memorable because it coincides with some snowy experiences from his youth, and perhaps from ours. The joy comes from the poet's words connecting to our sense of wonder or perhaps a kind of satisfaction with the match of his words and our emotions.

Service-learning is another approach that meets social and spiritual goals. For example, visiting elderly persons as a class with gifts of music and recitation brings joy to all. The psychomotor experience of moving outside the classroom walls is not to be underrated. Collateral learning is a new appreciation and respect for older, wiser human beings, not as objects for separation and misunderstanding, which is often the case for young people with limited vistas. Teachers can model respect. Joy comes from giving.

The caveat for teachers who sometimes enjoy their students too much (who might overdo the affective and psychomotor) is to seek balance, just as Bloom and his associates inferred. The balance is the holistic combination of academic, affective (social and spiritual), and psychomotor curriculum and methodology that results in transformational learning. Joy in learning is in itself a counter-balance to what is often a plodding, relentlessly predictable daily dose of standardized academic education.

> **Final Thoughts**
>
> Joy is there to be rediscovered in our classrooms. Our age of standardized schooling by its unbalanced nature shouts to us who will listen to teach to transform learners academically, socially, and spiritually. Voices like Bloom's and Gardner's are metaphorically imploring us that our students need a balanced diet of cognitive/affective/psychomotor experiences and an opportunity of perceiving learners as gifted with multiple talents/intelligences.
>
> Joy matters in schooling because of students like Kami, who in following her family dream found an educator who encouraged her spiritual essence. As many teachers know, we can invite joy just by being there for students who are seeking authority and support for who they are.
>
> We do not sacrifice standards as we seek to make learning fun for students. The vessel of creativity can assist us in incorporating joy in learning. Storytelling and reading books to children are research-based ways to touch and transform learners' lives. Eagerness to learn is innate and can be promoted by integrating authentic learning practices, including service learning, encouraging process over products in learning, modeling teacher sensitivity, providing constructive feedback, and building psychologically warm and supportive learning environments.

8

Prioritizing Relationships

Myth # 8	Fact # 8
Technological advances in this century demonstrate how less than essential teachers are.	Students need teachers' assistance in learning. The process of learning requires the organization, insightful challenges, feedback, and motivation provided by good teachers. Technology can assist but is not a substitute for teacher–student relationships.

The reader can readily note that this chapter is entitled "Prioritizing Relationships" and not "technological advances in schools" or "computers as teacher substitutes." Educators generally do not fear losing their jobs to digitation as much as they fear the dangers of social media, excessive screen time, and artificial intelligence (AI) for their students. They also are anxious as how to cope educationally with the newest of technology's demands. To paraphrase Ben Franklin, if we do not keep our heads we will surely lose them to the vicissitudes of technology. We can keep our heads by not losing our hearts.

Perspective: Consider the Contrast!

Two veteran middle-school teachers "in a shared journey" for 32 years in Grand Blanc, MI, interviewed with a local newspaper (*Flint Journal*, 2025), with Kimberly Locher teaching eighth-grade ELA and Deborah Lacki teaching/leading seventh and eighth grade Science. Inside their classrooms a 22-year-old Sulcata African tortoise named Gil roams freely as a beloved mascot and enhancer of the family atmosphere the two educators have created. Each teacher talks about fostering connection and curiosity among their students, and how important it was for them to create *routine*, especially for classroom management after the disruption of COVID-19. One speaks of how she was forced to grow technology-wise and considers herself the better teacher for it. And, they stress how vital it is to fight the feeling that "kids can't fail. It is OK for a child to get a low grade and then grow from it. I hope parents can trust us… Kids need humans… I had a tough time in middle school as a student, so I connect with these kids" (p. 7). Contrast this anecdote with a story about an online charter school in Arizona (Schultz, 2025) entitled, "This School Will Have Artificial Intelligence Teach Kids (With Some Human Help)." The school's model prioritizes AI in its delivery of core academics with the teachers serving as, and known as, "guides." The guides are there for motivation and emotional support, while AI is the teaching engine for content. The ratio is one guide to 33 students. The guides will teach communication, teamwork, and leadership.

The model is a reaction to COVID-19 as well, but also to the teaching shortage in U.S. schools (largely caused, from this author's standpoint, by a decade of standardization of schooling). Note that this model replaces the teacher-scholar role with AI, but keeps, somewhat with humans the practitioner and relater roles. While this charter school movement might be an outlier, it may portend other macro-level efforts to apply advanced technology to pedagogy. We might watch carefully how policymakers and business leaders in education attempt to dehumanize schooling in the name of "efficiency" and with reverential curtsies to the latest in technology. Transformational educators' vigilance is needed!

Living with Technology

In a *Wall Street Journal* article (2025), Randazzo et al. interviewed teachers, some of whom think online tools help more personalized instruction, and others who say that a "screen-heavy approach has distracted students and burned out teachers" (p. 1) They quote Stephanie Galvani, a middle school English teacher in suburban Boston, "Covid really shifted things toward, "Oh, we can do this, but we didn't ask: 'Should we do this'" (p.1)? Technology, even AI, can never replace transformational teachers because only humans can transform other human learners. It takes a whole teacher to transform the whole child. The idea that a machine can replace a teacher reflects something deeper than the wonder of modern technology. It reflects a "jug to mug" philosophy of pedagogy.

The authors report that U.S. students in grades 1–12 spend an average of 98 minutes on school computers each school day, more than 20% of the average teaching time (based on data from Lightspeed Systems, a software company). A San Antonio eighth-grader says, "I don't like having my eyes glued on a screen for a while. It gives you a headache and I really lose my focus" (p. 1). Recent data confirms (Duarte, 2023) that teens are on screens more than seven hours a day, including after school. In a Seattle school system (Bryan, 2025), digital mathematics instruction has encountered decidedly mixed results in middle schooling. Students are missing essential hands-on learning under the guidance of practitioners who know that computer numeration and graphics cannot replace manipulative objects like base-ten blocks.

The contrast above highlights that we must always put technology in context, especially as it impacts the educational lives of our children. Is technology now a "crucial element in enhancing teaching and learning experiences" as some claim (Burns, 2024, p. 2)? Perhaps it is. We must remember that technology by definition is an application of scientific knowledge for practical purposes. It has come to be thought of as hardware and software designed to make our lives more convenient and efficient. "Convenient" means easier access and less effort. "Efficient" means time-saving and better organized.

The context is that technology *can* be convenient and efficient—we all *can* benefit from it. I am writing this book with its practical assistance and that makes me happy. The human irony is that anything that brings us a degree of happiness as human beings is potentially addictive, even unto the strong temptation toward dishonesty. We all should allow at least some pause, some expressed fear about the role of technology in young people's lives especially. Smartphones are small portable computers that are wonderfully convenient and efficient. Generation Z has likely been impacted more than any other group, but we all know the fears realized with social media. The new morality is to single out perceived offenders and bash them because "they deserve it." It is a fear realized that schools have to deal with in cyber bullying and shunning.

Perspective: AI

AI is not only potentially as impactful as the internet or smartphones on the historical lists of mass communication, it is a game changer in convenience, efficiency, and fearsome potential. There is no choice with it—we dare not ignore it because it is here, like looking in a mirror each day. To quote a comic strip philosopher, "We have met the enemy and he is us." AI will enable us to "work smarter, not harder," to use an overused term. Artificial Intelligence as an industry (Price, 2024) could be compared to the ancient Greek story of Prometheus where humankind received the gift and curse of fire, where in the 21st century, it is a new form of fire. And, in this case mortals not gods are in charge of the fire. The estimate is that two-thirds of U.S. high schoolers are using AI in some form of cheating. If this estimate is anywhere close to accurate, how can educators meet this challenge? The question with AI and any technology past, present, or future should be, what role will we allow it to play in educationally transforming the lives of students? Clarity of purpose and function is needed. Notice that this is a different question than what we typically see addressed, which is, how can AI make our lives easier as an educators?

Making the profession easier for teachers is a good thing, of course, because good teaching is difficult. Dueck (2025) details how ChatGPT can be used by teachers to unpack learning standards. AI is more of a conversation than a search, because while Google finds existing information, "ChatGPT makes it up as we go along—it's generative" (p. 3). Teachers can ask AI to generate helpful summaries, for example, in Dueck's description of how to approach a specific standard by prompting it with wording from the standard, like,

> I am a 9th grade science teacher, and I want to explore the following topic with my students: Investigate the

characteristic properties of metals, nonmetals, and metalloids, and classify elements according to these properties ... Moments after I pressed the "enter" key, I got a brief introduction and several bullet points under each of the key terms.

(p. 7)

Interestingly, AI-generated guidance may be wrong (as noted by ChatGPT beneath its search bar) and must be scrutinized by knowledgeable educators.

Cancer researchers use AI as a structural organizer to evaluate CAR T-cell therapy strategies (St. Jude *Inspire*, 2024). Any technology that productively assists in difficult tasks or research is beneficial. AI used by wise educators in the right context, with the teacher clearly in charge as a leader in the classroom, has great potential, for example, in generating questions for a planned discussion or speeding the search for visuals in a lesson or even creating draft templates for parental emails. One of my favorite benefits of AI is to ask it to organize an address I have written (me not AI) into three main points. Amazing convenience! But AI technology must not ever be mistaken for a relationship.

Good teaching has always begun with an attitude of integrity. The root word of integrity means "whole" or "complete," which is who we are/what we are when we are honest. When we are honest we are a whole person who respects the people in the world around us. So we must ask ourselves, what is my attitude, my goal, my mission as I approach school each day and walk into my classroom? Relationships must be primary.

The Teacher-Relater

The transformational teacher's role of *relater* is crucial to the success of making learning applications which connect and transform. The relater is the third leg of the teacher-role triangle, buttressing the scholar and the practitioner. Relational teachers are concerned about not just academic goals, but social and spiritual ones as well. Most teachers at all levels, I have found, focus more on the scholar and practitioner roles likely for a few reasons: (1) They think that these two roles require more intentionality in work and improvement. Thus, most of our professional development efforts are invested here; (2) Similarly, teachers take the relater role as a given in the makeup of their personality, viewing relational teaching as something they do not have to work at or nurture; and (3) In fact, some actually view a more caring persona in teachers as a weakness—viewing it as related to less rigor in a practitioner. So here is an important message for everyone: Research (Davis, 2003; Furrer & Skinner, 2003) shows that students who believe their teachers really care about them and support their efforts are more eager to engage and master subject matter.

Perspective: Hidden Curriculum

Julia is a kindergarten teacher who enjoys her job for multiple reasons. She loves young children; she feels up to the challenge of teaching profound concepts at five-year-olds' levels of development (a very "Bruner-like" concept); and Julia deeply year-after-year wants to make herself worthy of being children's first schoolteacher. The latter role is a particularly responsible one because not only are the students new to the system, but the parents and guardians are, too. Sometimes she finds herself part of what has been called the "hidden curriculum," a useful term for describing events like bus rides, cafeteria experiences, and school hallway bustle which educate students as much or more than planned classroom curricula. For example, one of her students fell ill in September and required a hospital stay. Julia was quite fresh from meeting both the child and the family but nevertheless took the time to visit her hospitalized kindergarten student one evening. The simple act of kindness and care, this attitude of integrity, left an indelible impression on the little girl and family. We all realize that human presence speaks loudly in times of crisis.

Now consider a contrast. Core standards have made their way into kindergarten classrooms along with an organizational structure of teaching specialists in first through third grades (middle childhood grades have long had specialists as teachers). The attending theory, what Bruner called "folk pedagogy," is that young students will benefit from the academic wealth of teachers who are strong in teaching reading and mathematics, subjects that are tested annually as low as the third grade in many states. Kincaid's (2022) writing for the National Council on Teacher Quality summarizes research in Indiana (Hwang &

Kisida, 2021) with fourth graders showing that teacher specialization in the early elementary grades leads to less teacher effectiveness. Student learning gains declined significantly in both reading and math. Disadvantaged students showed even greater negative impact. Other studies in North Carolina and Texas also showed negative impact on student achievement. The issue here is the weakening of teacher–student relationships.

This study and others perhaps demonstrate Bruner's point that intuitive belief, in this case that teacher specialization at all schooling levels should increase achievement, is not a reliable basis for school practice. No strong evidence was found that increasing the proportion of teacher specialists generates quality achievement, but schools have implemented primary grade specialization anyway. In fact, the evidence seems strong that disadvantaged young students suffer most from the lack of one teacher's quantity of attention in self-contained classrooms. The assertion here coincides with Frey et al. (2019) that all learning is social and emotional.

Kris, an elementary teacher now school leader, shares:

> Desiring to be relational, if nothing more, directs my thought pattern and my speech pattern. When a student keeps putting his head down, I quietly ask why; when a student speaks sharply, I quietly ask why; when a student doesn't have homework, I quietly ask why. More often than not, I get the "rest of the story": Mom and Dad were fighting, so I couldn't sleep; I was supposed to see my Dad, but he never showed up; I went to my Dad's last night and my homework is at my Mom's. That's not exactly individualized instruction, but perhaps it is relational teaching; at least I hope it's a start.

Relationships have always been vital in life and education, but the loneliness of our present age (where social media often substitutes for human relationships) seems to mandate a new awareness. It is more critical than ever that teachers, *in loco parentis* for 7 hours a day, 180 days a year in most states, fill a void that is expanding in our information age.

Perspective: "Darker Emotions Attract More Eyeballs"

Cal Newport (2019) in his book, *Digital Minimalism*, says, "In an open marketplace for attention, darker emotions attract more eyeballs than positive and constructive thoughts. For heavy internet users, repeated interaction with this darkness can become a source of draining negativity" (p. 16). I am hardly a Luddite or have jumped an anti-technology shark in education. In fact, the internet can be a wonderful source for topical research in schools. But I do know that young people desperately need teachers and other adults who model the authority of good relationships. Trusting authority is a human predisposition and a major way we learn, and adolescents especially must be able to surround themselves with bastions of support like teachers, parents, coaches, church leaders, and friends. Transformation through human relations is a higher calling than darkness and fear. Renowned social cognitivist Albert Bandura (2006) refers to *agency* as the capability to influence our own behavior as well as others' functions. We as teachers can influence others individually, through proxy in using others' means and knowledge (like school counselors or respected community members), and by collectively pooling a group of students to influence for good (like service-learning or food bank drives).

Embracing human interaction with confidence builds agency. Frey et al. (2019) say agency is "our capacity to act in empowered and autonomous ways. Beliefs about our agency influence confidence and contribute to our resiliency when faced with a negative event" (p. 20). The authors pair agency with *identity*, which they define as an understanding of who we are, including our talents and our shortcomings. They emphasize that a sense of agency is constructed by interaction with others. And, that *social capital*, students' social networks of family, friends, and community is a strong influence on agency because "their network of relationships keeps them feeling emotionally and psychologically safe" (p. 21). When we feel safe, we also feel more comfortable in taking risks in learning. And, with risk comes more confidence and perseverance.

Winston Churchill famously urged the British people in May 1940, as Hitler had declared war on them, "To never give up. Never, never, never." Teacher-of-the-year in her district, Sarah, and her student have similar values:

> How I can be a better teacher and teach to the whole student? We've reached a time in the school year when

all we're told is to review and prepare for the year-end test. While it is necessary to prepare students for it, I am frustrated that there is so much emphasis on it. Yesterday, my sweet dyslexic student was crying and frustrated during a required practice test. She is smart, funny, kind, and one of the hardest working students I've had. She has to work twice as hard as other students to overcome so many things, and yet she never gives up. The annual test won't measure how much she's grown this year or any of the amazing qualities she has. I remind her and my other students that they are amazing. My goal for them this year is to grow and be better students and people. I hope to give them something that will carry with them to and through middle school, not just a test score.

Education as a Moral Endeavor

Renowned educator John Goodlad (Goodlad et al., 1993) argued that teaching has a moral dimension because education is a moral endeavor, that teachers have a first responsibility to those being taught, which is a moral burden shared with parents and guardians. Schooling must be about relationships and feelings and beliefs, not just the addition of knowledge or new information. Knowing is bedrock, but believing can transcend knowing. And, believing for learners can be encouraged by teachers who seize the moral authority to prize students' individuality. It is not an authority that has to be ceded in the name of following district and state authorities' drive for high test scores. Unfortunately in today's school cultures, at least in many of them, state departments of education do seize such authority in the name of standardized accountability. Sarah, teacher-of-the-year elementary teacher, continues in a lament:

> Teachers are asked to use a new, scripted teaching program with fidelity because someone in authority says it yields great results for all students. Principals are asked to observe and ensure teachers are using the program each day. Teachers are also encouraged to push aside science and social studies if they are not tested or if it

is a year for a pilot test in a particular subject. We have forgotten about what really matters for the sake of what promises to bring great test scores.

This authority is currently meekly accepted by most parents as well. They and the school should have a partnership in the education of the young. But as Sarah adds:

> Many times parents see education as the school's responsibility, but by that same token, some schools give up on trying to involve parents and carry the weight of educating the student all alone.

The reason schools often give up on parental involvement is because they know parents are busy, in fact busier than ever. They want to help busy parents, and they think they can do that by "going it alone" in the partnership. In addition, school communities, which are by definition educators and parents, currently see the highest authority as "achievement-driven" not "person-driven." This is and always has been a fundamental mistake in education because people-focused education leads to higher achievement. Why sacrifice something so vital so needlessly?

Thus, many schools and educators take on the whole weight of educating children; and, they do it with a sole-achievement mantra. How do we turn this around? We should first recognize and then adamantly assert that we teachers have a responsibility to attend to their students' social well-being and to their individual potential. Frey et al. (2019) say it this way:

> Based on these experiences (working with thousands of educators and students across the grades) and on our review of the research, we have concluded that because teachers unquestionably influence students' social and emotional development, they have a responsibility to do so in a way that is positive and deliberate.
>
> (p. 4)

This conclusion is well supported by social cognitive theorists (Bandura, 1986; Rosenthal & Zimmerman, 1978) who say that much of human learning involves observing and interacting with other people. Cognitivists in general study mental phenomena like memory, perception, problem solving, and more, meaning they study the *relationship of things we can see to things we cannot see.* Relationships affect achievement.

Other theorists in the tradition of Lev Vygotsky say that student relationships in learning and development are affected by culture (Tomasello, 2019). This speaks to the role of the learning environment we create for our learners in the school and the classroom. These theorists emphasize human language enabling us to communicate and collaborate, and through our culture pass along a knowledge heritage to successive generations (Ormrod, 2012; Tomasello, 2019). This knowledge heritage is academic, social, and spiritual in goal structure.

What we say and do as teachers impacts emotions, the human spirit itself. Students are in the process of forming, of determining their identities. A transforming authority is needed. The role of teacher-relater is not an add-on to the other two roles of scholar and practitioner, as though the three roles are not all essential parts of the whole teacher. All three roles must synergize to reach the goal of transformation of learners.

Authority and Achievement

Frey et al. (2019) emphasize teachers' being "positive and deliberate" in developing social-emotional learning (SEL). Some might ask why such intentionality is critical. One reason is that social and spiritual goals are an end to themselves. The authors cite Durlack et al. (2011) who, in a meta-analysis, identified six factors in SEL that were impacted by teachers who implemented SEL teaching:

1. Social and emotional skills—e.g., interpersonal problem-solving, decision-making
2. Attitudes toward self and others—e.g., self-esteem, self-efficacy
3. Positive social behavior—e.g., getting along with others

4. Conduct problems—e.g., aggression, disruptive behavior, bullying
5. Emotional distress—e.g., depression, anxiety
6. Academic performance—e.g., reading and mathematics achievement scores (p. 7)

Note that the first five factors fit in most definitions of SEL, but that academic performance was included in the study because it was positively impacted by teachers' SEL teaching. This leads to the second reason for intentional SEL teaching: *It absolutely stimulates students to learn more*. Both rationales seem important for why relational teaching is significant, but the first one, that social and spiritual goals are an end in themselves, endures.

Perspective: Subversive Activity

Elementary school teacher Terri says that "I hope my administration doesn't discover that I told my students that I care about them more than test scores." This same teacher reported great results to go with great relationships, just as research indicates. The teacher felt almost subversive in prioritizing relationships.

A trust relationship between teacher and students undergirds whole child education. Unfortunately there is evidence that in our achievement drive, the whole child can be lost. Learners' mistakes can be blown out of proportion and with their immaturity they fight to hold on to themselves.

Perspective: Hold onto Yourself

People want something and someone to believe in. Learners need to believe in and trust their teachers. And, we teachers must be worthy of that trust. A lack of a trust-relationship in the teacher–student dynamic can be telling. A way to counsel some self-regulation with children is to advise them privately (apart from peers) to literally "hold on" to themselves by positioning their arms in a self-hug whenever they feel let down by someone or something. Ask them to tell themselves "who they are" and to not let go until they can verbalize it. Be there and be sure the verbalizing is positive and reinforcing. Errors indeed can become an emotional "trial" with perceived nonsupportive teachers (and other adults and peers). But, all individuals can become overcomers if we hold onto who we are.

Most all of us know about the impact of embarrassment and disparagement intuitively as teachers, but neuroscience backs it up. Allison Posey (2019) writes about the two brain regions studied specifically for emotional responses: the *cingulate cortex* and the *amygdala*. She says the former acts "like a paintbrush, 'painting' an experience based on memories and emotions" (p. 40). The cingulate cortex is located in the medial prefrontal part of the cortex. If students have an embarrassing moment in a classroom, for example, this part of the brain stamps the memory. If the class environment is a "safe" one for students' making mistakes, the brain connects to positive emotions, thus informing motivation in the future. If the environment is negative with a critical teacher and/or peers, the whole experience is painted negatively for future motivation.

The amygdala is a small almond-shaped region buried deep in the brain, tagging emotional experiences and networking with other parts of the brain to enhance memory. Stress-related hormones are triggered by the amygdala, influencing memory systems such as the hippocampus, which is the organizing region of the inner brain. That embarrassing moment becomes a memory that our brain remembers. Posey says that "activation of emotion networks such as the amygdala and the cingulate cortex can motivate a learner's actions, with both conscious and unconscious awareness" (p. 40). The good news about our brains is that emotional ups and downs can be somewhat effectively mitigated by learners who are more self-directed.

The goal for every teacher at any level should be to inspire and create learners who can function with some freedom and independence. Teachers who have transformation as a goal can inspire and create truly independent learners. These self-directed learners are empowered to ask relevant questions about the information they receive. One of the most decisive times in students' lives is preadolescence. Rhonda Whitman (2019) writes about "three things middle schoolers need":

1. Positive adult–student relationships—Teachers should encourage students and families to seek out people at school concerning stressors they are encountering. Everyone working toward mutual goals can change a student's life.

2. Community connections—Students can be reminded that they are a part of something larger than themselves by inviting the community to participate in school events like literacy festivals. Adults can read aloud and share hobbies and expertise in school events. Students also can go out into communities with well-planned field trips. "These experiences help create lasting connections that extend beyond the school year" (p. 1).
3. Opportunities to explore interests by reading—Encouraging reading goes well beyond skills: "Literacy infuses essential skills including social emotional learning and critical thinking, preparing kids to be independent thinkers and active collaborators who can adapt to succeed in tomorrow's careers" (p. 1).

The relationships formed between teachers and learners are at the heart of teaching and learning. Teachers who prize this role relate all learnings to contemporary life so that the goal is transformation. One way of thinking about teacher-relaters is that they give social and spiritual context to information or knowledge.

Sabrina, now a school leader, reflects on her life as a teacher:

Perspective: Looking Back to Look Ahead

As I look back on my teaching and the things I loved most of about teaching, assessments do not make the list. I run into former students all the time and hear, "You were my favorite teacher." They will say, "Do you remember …" Not one time have they mentioned the number of assessments I gave them. What they mention is the relationships, the fun we had learning, and what we experienced together. I tried to always love my students first, motivate them, and provide experiences they could learn from. I had high expectations and I certainly wanted them to perform well on the test. Even then, it caused me a great deal of stress. I valued being an effective teacher.

The relationships formed between teachers and learners are at the heart of teaching and learning. Teachers who prize this role relate all learnings to contemporary life so that the goal is transformation. Teacher-relaters have attitudes of integrity.

How We Can Relate

Psychologist Carl Rogers (1969), whom I referenced earlier, gave us the term "facilitator of learning" in education. He was once asked to reflect upon what a great teacher is. In an address at Harvard he said he thought about the very best teachers he had ever had, and came to an abrupt conclusion. "Teacher" as a term connoted an information-giver to most people, or as he phrased it from a dictionary definition, "to teach is to make to learn." His reflection was that the best teachers made learning easier (facilitated) for their students by exhibiting three "attitudinal" qualities: *realness, empathy,* and *prizing*. Realness means we show them who we are. Empathy means we show them we care. Prizing means we show connection with them as individuals. Here are some "how's" to relating:

Realness or genuineness is a quality of educators who are not afraid to be themselves. Teacher-relaters are *real* by:

- Keeping all their emotions measured and under control, but they are not afraid to show the brain emotions of joy, anger, humor, and sadness in the classroom. Students can "relate" to such genuineness.
- Being the adult in the room (after all, teachers' evaluation role draws a line) while enjoying student-behavior on a human level.
- Letting students know they are persons by occasionally referencing home or friends or other "human-windows" that allow students to really see their teachers.
- Adoring their subject. Realness can be manifested in teachers' enthusiasm for their subject. Loving what we do is compelling to students.
- Exhibiting a genuineness when we use body language and encouraging words to prompt student interaction. Students feel a connection to "real" teachers.
- Letting students know beforehand that we like to use "pause time" after more reflective questions. This simple act of communication is a liberating classroom experience.

- Demonstrating our enthusiasm by placing inspiration before information as a priority. Meaning is enhanced which furthers engagement.
- Apologizing/Acknowledging when we are wrong. With confident teachers such realness is a great strength.

Empathy is perhaps the crown jewel of human-ness because it involves an open and understanding teacher heart. As teacher-relaters we can *empathize* by:

- Respecting our learners by keeping a modest tone, never condescending or sarcastic.
- Respecting our learners by praising their hard work and effort.
- Relating to students that we too have had certain feelings and made mistakes.
- Explaining carefully how (in a course or a unit) our students will be assessed.
- Giving students time to answer a question, or another chance to elaborate.
- Structuring our teaching so that learners have a variety a ways to succeed.
- Using more student-centered pedagogies that allow their participation.
- Grading essay questions conscientiously with *constructive* criticism.
- Communicating with students (and their parents) in a timely, open manner.
- Asking students to think deeply about a question or issue, and telling them it may be difficult.
- Organizing it so that students receive grades early, middle, and late in the term, instead of concentrating most everything at the end.
- Moderating homework assignments, especially in tandem with other teachers on school special event nights.

Prizing as a quality can make teachers literally unforgettable. "Who was your favorite teacher?" is an important question. Teachers who prize are usually the answer.

Perspective: Go to the Head of the Class

Many years ago a family box-game similar to "Trivial Pursuit" was popular. My fourth grade teacher, Mrs. Hobbes, invited me to bring the game called, "Go to the Head of the Class," to school one day because we were studying world geography and she knew the game had a whole section on that subject. My family had played the game many times at home before it ever went to school with me. My teacher knew this and thus did not include me in the "quizzing" competition of the game questions, only asking me for an answer after all others had missed. I may have known most of the answers, but what was important, was the joy of being prized! It was a forever experience. I still remember Tierra del Fuego, "an island off the southern tip of South America separated from the mainland by the Strait of Magellan named after the Portuguese explorer, sailing for Spain, who first circumnavigated the world." Later my curiosity led me to find that the island name, "Land of Fire," came from Ferdinand Magellan in 1520 who saw numerous bonfires of the indigenous Yaghan people (who were trying to keep warm) on the island. Little did I know that I would someday (1969) witness different explorers, American astronauts, the first to land on the cold, charcoal moon and return home, not to Spain or Portugal, but earth.

Mrs. Hobbes was not constrained by core standards and pacing guides to use her creative instincts in teaching geography to fourth graders. She had state guidelines setting ranges for time spent on math, English, science, history, and geography. That creative opportunity for that fourth-grade teacher made at least one student feel very special. It was indeed transformational learning.

Teacher-relaters *prize* their students by:

- Making them feel they are special "prizes." It is not favoritism. It is sensitive spotlighting.
  Some students will likely make you their all-time favorite teacher in response.
- Respecting them even more than a subject.
- Teaching them the subject, not teaching a subject to them. It is the students' perceived relationship that matters, not vice versa. Because teachers are authority figures, students want to know what their teachers think of them.
- Listening carefully by responding to their individual identity. Here a real connection can be made.
- Trying to listen more and talk less.

- ♦ Telling them that we want them to succeed and then allowing them to.
- ♦ Talking with them kindly outside of class time (as well as inside).
- ♦ Taking the time to make insightful, constructive comments on student essays.

Perspective: Prizing Students

To make a student feel like one of "our prizes" involves a bit of risk. What about the notion of equity and impartiality? Actually the concept of equity says that some students need the prizing more than others. The risk is to prize one may deflate another. A fifth-grader who thought she was prized was deflated when her teacher wrote a page of glowing remarks in a yearbook of another student but not in hers (teachers should not be writing in student yearbooks anyway). Every child has something special about them to be prized—that is the basis of sensitivity. Prize quietly, even unobtrusively. It is a spiritual goal. Spiritual is something we already are as relational humans, not something to be attained. Transformational teachers look for the good to privately reinforce it. Teacher-relaters meet both social and spiritual goals.

The power of the teacher-student relationship can be transformational. These educational times demand that we harness that power, and good relationships in the classroom are most effectively fostered by teachers who facilitate learning by serving all three roles of transformational teaching.

Final Thoughts

Technology and human relationships may seem like odd-fellows in this chapter. By definition the "application of science to knowledge for practical purposes" seems a far cry from relational teachers who connect to academic, social, and spiritual goals in a classroom. Technology should be approached with a healthy sense of context: It can truly assist but is not a substitute for teacher-student relationships."

Students who believe their teachers care for them are more eager to engage and master subject matter. The more ways we can find to enhance teacher–student relationships, the more we generate quality achievement. A salient pedagogical point in this book is the value of trial-and-error learning, the importance of allowing students to take risks without being embarrassed or punished for mistakes. When students feel safe with relational teachers and their supportive classroom environments, they feel more comfortable in taking risks in learning.

Teachers unquestionably influence learners' social and emotional development—doing so should be intentional and positively supportive. The authority of transforming teachers is needed to assist maturing students to develop strong identities. SEL factors include academic performance in their impact. Intentional SEL teaching absolutely stimulates students to learn more.

The goal of every teacher at any level is to inspire and create learners who function with some freedom and independence. The role of teacher-relater synergizes with the other two transformational roles of scholar and practitioner, giving social and spiritual context to knowledge. Relaters have at least three vital attitudinal qualities: realness, empathy, and prizing. And, each quality can manifest itself in very practical ways in our classrooms. The relationships formed between teachers and learners are at the heart of teaching and learning.

9

Securing Teacher Identity

Myth # 9	Fact # 9
Covering subject matter connected to rigorous standards is the most vital role of teachers.	Teaching for coverage is vastly overrated and mostly irrelevant. Teachers build their identity by serving many roles, and deserve recognition for their individual expertise.

Knowing and believing in ourselves, even being happy in what we do and think, means strong identity. It is extremely relevant in this time of standardized schooling to focus on teacher identity. One of the significant reasons for low teacher morale in our U.S. public schools, perhaps historically low, is because of unrecognized individual expertise. Great teachers can do great things if allowed to thrive. Teachers are as individual as their students in their strengths and needs.

Just as we talk about students as individuals who need singular and differentiated attention, we must recognize that teachers, who are entrusted with our nation's children and their learning seven hours daily every week, have compelling individual needs. Teachers need our support not our anger. Systems that force the role of coverage of standards linked to unbridled accountability as primary are systematically guilty of removal of teachers' individual creativity, and thus of threatening their very identity. Freedom to teach has become one of our nation's most urgent clarion calls.

One elementary teacher says,

> As long as my students produced the data points required by the district, my school was happy with me. The problem was I was not happy with myself because I knew that those same "points" were obstacles to my creatively reaching my students. I have had to learn to be more interactive within the confines of standards-based teaching.

Most research about teacher identity concerns, legitimately, professional identity. We cannot discuss professional identity, however, without including personal identity because they are rather inseparable. All of us who are happy in whatever job we occupy likely feel that way because someone that we work for or with not only believes in our professional skillset but also in us as human beings. Professional and personal values and beliefs go together. Most definitions of teacher identity include personal values, professional values, and our individual shaping from cultural experiences. The latter factor is "shaping" because it is our interaction with other people, particularly with others who might hold different worldviews, that give us social awareness and define who we are.

Perspective: Who They Were

Encouraging teachers (and students) to read well-written biographies of admired people can help us not only know who they were, but also who we are. Lincoln wrote a short speech on an envelope on a train bound for Gettysburg. His address commemorated the horrific battle that occurred there while placing it in the context of the founding of America, "four score and seven years ago." He spoke for 3 minutes and used 272 elegant words. A little over a century later another man spoke at the National Cathedral in our nation's capital four days before his death. Martin Luther King echoed national unity (and some of his words years earlier from a jail cell) by saying, "We Americans are tied together in the single garment of destiny, caught in an inescapable network of mutuality. And whatever affects one directly affects all indirectly . . ." M.L.K. called us to do right with justice and alleviate poverty as a nation. Lincoln was a wise but secular speaker while King was a minister. Both men's lives can assist in telling us who we are.

Defining ourselves with individual "social shaping" is an integral part of Vygotsky's (1978) socioculturalism. For him learning is a universal part of developing organized human social-emotional function. His "zone of proximal development" was the "distance between the actual development level ... and the level of potential development" (p. 86). This theory applies, not just to learning but also to teaching as a cultural activity where educators learn from each other in communities (Wenger, 1998). With identity, what is our "actual" as compared to our "potential" development?

Perspective: Teacher Identity

As a middle school mathematics teacher I learned many things about myself. For the first time I was

(1) encountering students who were in great flux about who they were as human beings; and
(2) working with a team of professionals who had far richer cultural experiences than I as it related to teaching. I learned then, and continue to learn, that diversity in all its forms is a part of our world, and that my role as a teacher is one of the few authoritative props for support that our schoolchildren have. I learned that I was inadequate to the task in terms of teacher identity, and made it my goal to change.

Teacher identity is such a crucial topic in education because it affects everything that teachers do, which affects everything that students can be, which is the essence of transformational teaching and learning.

Guiding Stars for Identity

Whether identity is applied to an individual or an organization, it is vital that it is first recognized and then developed. Organizations often set "core values" or a "codes of ethics" as guiding stars for their identity as an organization or agency. Perhaps we should do the same as educators. What are our guiding stars in education? As teachers in these stressful times, it is even more important to know who we are as individuals. There is nothing standardized about human individuality. In all humility teachers must shout to themselves, "I've got a name!" Sometimes it seems for busy teachers that they spend so much of their time serving others that they forget to develop a strong sense of who they are. Other times we forget whom we are serving and lose ourselves. It is our balance of attitudinal qualities. Teachers often feel exhausted at the end of a school day not so much from physical exertion but from emotional energy spent. If we want to have a transformational identity, we can develop some "core values" like these:

1. Develop a meta-cognitive mindset. We must think about our thinking at the end of each day or perhaps each week. Keeping an identity-journal where we *briefly* record what we did and said and what our students did and said can be revealing.
2. Look for attitudes that reflect conforming and nonconforming patterns within the standardized culture. Adopt mindsets of detachment as we observe. Then engage. All educators must conform to a certain degree in order to keep their jobs in this age of micromanagement of teachers' freedom to teach. Conformity can be as simple as following the rules, which is a good thing for both the individual and the system. However, in every organization whether it is schooling or business, leaders can quietly stand up for their principles on behalf of those they serve.
3. Record a teacher-mantra in writing where we can routinely look at it, like, "What I believe makes a difference!" Put it on a sticky note or wear it on a bracelet. Be meta-spiritual. Make it a point to meditate on it especially during the "testing season" of February-April.
4. Hire and follow school leaders who care about the whole learner. It can make all the difference in our school cultures by adopting a transformational identity. This means communicating constantly that we are serving students' transformation with a long-term, life-long mindset. Standardized schooling will pass away soon we hope, but educators who serve learners' greatest needs are making an eternal difference.

Great teachers have always occupied more than a pedagogical role as part of their identity. It is the most defining role, but we all know that teachers routinely serve as counselors, technology consultants, parental advisors, paper shufflers, evaluators, and more. Part of the "more" is test results-indicators or barometers for their school, a role teachers should not have to play, as discussed earlier. Teachers are there for learners. Within the pedagogy role, standardized education has increasingly foisted upon teachers the role of lockstep coverage of content framed by standards. It is a zero-sum game, defeating good teachers before they even start.

Coverage

Teaching for coverage of a set of standards is a role imposed on teachers in standardized school systems. Covering a subject instead of, for example, allowing students to plumb the depths of a topical area is not only overrated but also a vast waste of time. Coverage-teaching is mostly irrelevant because by definition it only skims the surface of the curriculum before moving on to the next standard. It is probably the easiest kind of teaching we do and, deservedly, the least effective. Coverage-teaching effectively suspends the practitioner role. Requiring teaching-to-the-test coverage is demeaning to the identities of educators who know they can be and do so much more. Students do not learn when depth and meaning are ignored. Teachers need freedom to think "less is more," fewer topics with more depth.

Perspective: Postholing

Perhaps solutions are there for us to see if we look. In another writing (Rosebrough & Leverett, 2011), I compared good teaching to beautifully constructed white fences on the green grass of a horse farm. We admire the perimeter of the fencing but the posts are responsible for their endurance. Digging deep for sturdiness is a metaphor for good theory into practice: Teachers in their pedagogy will find that regularly "postholing" to deepen knowledge and understanding is vastly superior to mile wide-inch deep instruction we call coverage (McTighe et al., 2004; Schwartz et al., 2008). Students who study fewer topics with more depth are more positively, significantly affected

> in learning. It is brain-science that our dendrites need meaning to grow into neural networks, and students need depth to find that meaning, and digging takes time. Taking the time pays learning dividends later.

As an example let us choose a specific subject for further emphasis. As most school people realize, no disciplinary area in today's schools suffers more from lack of attention than the teaching of history. Traditionally, this subject has likely also suffered from coverage-teaching the most, resulting in history-hating learners. Annie Brown (Ferlazzo, 2019), a Los Angeles high school humanities teacher and curriculum coach, blogs about engaging students in the process of inquiring about history:

> Instead of viewing history as facts to memorize, we should think of history as the complex and competing interpretations of those facts resulting from a careful examination of historical evidence. This means less focus on information and more focus on process. Approaching history through inquiry can alleviate other challenges social studies teachers face: Instead of the mad dash to cover an endless number of topics (which can be overwhelming to students and teachers), teachers can select topics that they see as generative, engaging, and relevant to big questions facing society today. If you teach with essential questions, you have the seeds of inquiry in your curriculum.
>
> (p. 2)

It is little wonder that social studies when taught badly is often students' least favorite subject area (it is also the least standardized-tested area). Amy Okimoto, third grade teacher in Colorado, says in her blog (Ferlazzo, 2019):

> In my home state of Colorado, teaching social studies at the elementary level has all but fallen by the wayside in many districts, mine included. Increased emphasis on literacy at the primary grades, resulting from state legislation (READ Act, to be specific) has forced social studies instruction out the door. When most social studies instruction does

> take place, it is lacking in high levels of engagement, thus missing the opportunity to empower and excite students... Teachers instead should fully embrace the concept that social studies is not simply maps and history but instead the rich connections between humans, resources, and land, and how those interactions have shaped history.
>
> (p. 1)

Often our mistake in teaching social studies is that we fail to emphasize the "social." History is about people like us, and not like us. The social relevance is built in for our learners, but meaning is lost when depth is lacking. Teaching for coverage is checking the goal-and-objective boxes without stopping to check for understanding. It is not to be confused with more lecture-oriented approaches, which when coupled with a monitor-and-adjust interaction, can be fruitful pedagogy.

> Jerome Bruner in his classic, *The Process of Education* (1960), wrote:
>
> To instruct someone... is not a matter of getting him (her) to commit results to mind. Rather, it is to teach him (her) to participate in the process that makes possible the establishment of knowledge. We teach a subject not to produce little living libraries on that subject, but rather to get a student to think mathematically for himself, to consider matters as an historian does, to take part in the process of knowledge-getting. Knowing is a process not a product.
>
> (p. 72)

Asking teachers to primarily fill the role of teaching for coverage is what Bruner might term product-oriented teaching. Fulfilling this role week after week can lead to morale problems.

Teacher Methodology and Morale

Kurtz et al. (2024) introduced a "Teacher Morale Index" to measure year-to-year teacher enthusiasm and confidence.

From a public school workforce of 3 million, teachers have for the last few years "reported high levels of burnout and disillusionment" (p. 1). Their inaugural overall index score is –13 on a scale from –100 to +100. Below zero obviously represents lower morale and above zero indicates higher morale. Thus, teachers in 2023–2024 are feeling more negatively about their jobs.

The highest score is +1 among foreign language teachers. The lowest score is –21 among elementary teachers and science/social studies teachers at –21. Mathematics and computer science teachers weigh in at –3, English/reading at –7, PE at –6, special education teachers are at –14, and fine arts at –19.

Where teachers' work impacts scores: urban at –22, suburban at –16, town at –12, and rural at –2. The "strongest" morale is among Black teachers at +5, Hispanic at –6, Mixed race at –11, and White at –13. Teachers' scores varied according to career stage: less than 3 years at +4, 3–9 years at –20, 10–20 years at –11, and more than 20 years at –12.

The research, as we know, is strong in saying that the critical element of engaging students and transforming classroom environments is the teacher. But teachers are human beings with emotions and intellect. Most teachers are there because they want to have creative ownership of their classroom. Trying new ways to reach all students is a creative challenge that most teachers embrace.

Our students deserve to see us as a work in progress in leaving no teaching role neglected. The roles of scholar and practitioner and relater can flow from an effort to achieve balance and holism. Generally we can observe teachers who fulfill one or two of these roles. It is uncommon (unfortunately) for teachers to fulfill all three, but a worthy goal. Some enter teaching because they love their subject. Some find teaching a fulfilling career because they are effective in orchestrating ways and methods of connecting to learners. And, some are born people-persons who really care about their students individually. Each role is worthy of respect by those who study pedagogy. Teachers can spend their teaching lives on the satisfying journey of fulfilling and synergizing these three roles.

Balance in Mutuality

Teachers make hundreds of decisions, big and little, every day. The biggest ones, seemingly, involve application of their scholarship and pedagogy. The smallest ones, which can become big because they are attitudinal as a teacher-relater, include patience, clarity, and empathy. Decision-making is aided by strong teacher identity which can make life much simpler in a classroom as we seek to transform learners.

Teachers are as unique as their students, and need to be recognized for not just what they do but for who they are. Identity for teachers crosses the students' stream of identity, too. Mutual transformation is real, just as Hargreaves et al. (2024) remind us that "student engagement and teacher engagement are not islands in a stream" (p. 14). The challenge of transformational learning in this era of schooling can demand our all, forcing critical self-examination. We all gain our identities from comparing ourselves to others, but we also need to aspire to standards we can set for ourselves.

Perspective: Personal Balance

Here I think balance in our personal lives is crucial because, as I related above, personal identity is an inseparable part of professional identity. I recall listening on a "radio drive" years ago to a psychologist, in retrospect to what we now call a positive psychologist (I do not recall his name), who said keep your life simple by seeking a balance of four areas: love, work, play, and worship. Obviously each of the four areas can mean something different for different people, but I took the advice to heart. I began to realize that when one of the areas, like work for example, gets too heavy or too "important," that my life would veer off balance. I would then consciously seek to become more self-aware of another area that perhaps was suffering from inattention, like finding ways to love my family more.

One of the themes in this book is knowing our students. And, to know our students we must know ourselves (Socrates would approve!). Jessica, an elementary school educator, thinks about her impact, finding balance in mutuality:

To teach is to influence life change. I have had teachers who changed my life for the better. I have had teachers who changed my life for the worse. In fact, I have had both types of experiences as both student and as an adult through my career. We must always remember the impact we have on our students. Caring for the social-emotional needs of our students as well as the academic needs is crucial for their continuing engagement in learning and for their future role in society. We must build relationships with our students, model openness, cultivate trust, and risk vulnerability. Education should be a "mutually transforming experience" that improves the lives of all involved.

Teacher Efficacy

Knowing ourselves as professionals begins with knowing why we are serving as educators. We learned early in teacher preparation that *knowing why* begins with a philosophy of education. A philosophy for teachers is like holding a lantern to light our path. It illuminates every decision we make relating to education inside (instruction) and outside (planning) the classroom. Knowing our philosophy informs who we are as professionals and helps to build an incredibly vital teacher quality: self-confidence. Maintaining confidence may mean changing to a brighter lantern light.

Every grade level has its challenges, but to choose one for illustration, consider middle-school teachers. Students at the preadolescence age are seeking to discover who they are, and they demonstrate daily their identity-journey like the peaks and valleys of an electrocardiogram. The electrical signals of teachers' hearts can coincide! They often realize how inadequate they are to the task at hand. Middle school demands a strong sense of identity in teachers. "Monitoring" instruction and adapting to the personal and pedagogical needs in their classroom requires a steadiness that can only come from confident self-knowledge. We as transformational teachers have high expectations for our students, believing, really believing they can succeed. Educational psychologists say such teachers are high-efficacy (Bruning et al., 2011).

Perspective: High-Efficacy Teachers

Teacher efficacy as a term has been used since the early 1990s. There are high-efficacy teachers and there are low ones. High-efficacy teachers have a greater sense of personal accomplishment and convey more positive expectations to their students. They use more teaching strategies, spend more time on academic accountability, and show more confidence in consulting with parents (Egyed & Short, 2006). How do we increase teacher efficacy? Administrative support is vital along with more focus on teacher planning (Alderman, 2004). School administration can encourage good relationships among teachers. And, teachers who are more systematic in planning for learners' improvement enhance their efficacy. Confidence is often lacking with newer teachers—it will come with time if preparation is a priority. And, as Wise and Pandolpho (2019) remind us, school leaders can help them understand that "they can compensate . . . with their abundance of passion and enthusiasm" (p. 25).

Consider year-beginning open houses and parent-teacher meetings at school. Trending now in some schools are "celebration of back-to-school" parties among new students and school personnel. Most students are excited to meet their new teachers, especially in the elementary and middle grade years. Parents, to be fair, are apprehensive as well as curious about their children's beginning school at any level. Some have serious frustration and are disappointed. What about teachers? They of course have some of these same feelings: excitement, apprehension, curiosity, frustration, and disappointment. Teachers are trained to be professional and show positive emotions despite what might be happening in their home life, but they cannot be "trained" vto be confident and independent. They earn these qualities through experience with support. Thus, teachers can have their own self-efficacy issues.

Some teachers may try to compete with a peer down the hall in terms of personality or teaching style. Some don't try to compete at all to a fault: They exhibit a take-it-or-leave-it attitude because they are weary from trying to please. They quit early and fail. Others are confident in who they are, believe in themselves, and realize that students and parents need their expertise and inspiration—the very definition of high self-efficacy. In this "positive psychology" realm is where we educators must try to understand our counselor role and focus on attitudes and interpersonal skills. Self-efficacy embraces risk in addressing social-emotional goals like mental health and wellness, a vital part of knowing our students. Happy, confidant, caring teachers spur learning and achievement.

In education we can race and easily lose track of who we are and what we are doing. Teacher identity involves feeling free, feeling autonomous. Today's schools can hardly reach for the stars when even trying something innovative in a classroom is more difficult than it should be. Breaking from a routine or a comfort zone, which is part of trial-and-error learning, must be rewarded not punished!

Perspective: Risk Not Rewarded

Maria, a middle school teacher, fears change because of the emphasis on teacher assessment. She sometimes feels like she sits in a classroom fishbowl with numerous visitors trekking in and out all day as they observe and assess. Spontaneity in teachable moments is not rewarded in Maria's culture. Whatever is done must be planned and scripted—which is not a bad thing necessarily because planning and teaching to outcomes are important. But, when we take away teachers' zeal and creativity, we take away some of their heart and soul as well. Thus, we codify entrenchment.

Students have these issues as well. Teachers' having agency makes a difference in whether they transform learners or not. Optimism and high expectations and growth mindset can be communicated. And, connecting to individual students must be intentional. It turns out that a significant part of feeling autonomous is *recognition*. Students have these issues as well.

Perspective: Loneliness in Teen Culture

Loneliness can come to everyone, including our students. Feeling recognized for who we really are is an important part of life. Sima Sistani, co-founder of the group video-chat "Houseparty," said in an interview with *Wall Street Journal's* Future of Everything Festival (Gee, 2019) that millennial and Gen Z kids are on the precipice of a loneliness epidemic. The root cause is how people communicate on instant-messaging services and social-media posting asynchronous messages whenever it is convenient. Teens have a lot more alone time as they group text-message threads with many sets of friends at once, but not necessarily in real time. It is efficient but "it doesn't fill your tank in the same way that seeing somebody face to face does. The last decade was about sharing, the next decade will be about participating" (p. 2). Thus, schooling can assist with such loneliness by creating classroom pedagogies, like guided inquiry teaching and small group discussion, that bring human communication and individual recognition back into connectivity. Group work when done well can foster civility qualities and diminish loneliness itself. Civility is a learned behavior. Loneliness should not be school-inflicted.

The Role of Recognition

Everyone wants to be recognized in some way. Some need it less than others, but all human beings need recognition as a kind of affirmation. As teachers we understand the importance of "recognizing" our students. We know their names; we read and comment on their work (as termed "feedback"); we celebrate their individuality. Teaching is love translated to our students through our words and actions in classrooms. But what about teachers?

High teacher morale among all experience levels is an enormous part of teacher effectiveness.

Perspective: You Haven't Lived Until . . .

Lew Wallace lived his life in the latter part of the 19th century. He was best known as a Union general at the Battle of Shiloh, but he had many accomplishments after the American Civil War, including writing *Ben-Hur*, the best-selling religious novel of that century, made into an Academy Award winning motion picture in the 20th century. Wallace believed that a person had not lived a full life unless he or she had: (1) published a book; (2) learned to play a musical instrument; (3) painted a piece of art; or (4) patented an invention. I'm sure he was sincere, but we can add to this list. Teachers can transform lives if they seek holism in their roles. Is this not part of a full life for teachers? The difference perhaps from Wallace's list is that many educators work in communities that currently stifle full growth. A question remains: How can we reinvent schools to inspire full lives?

We cannot allow others to tell us we are unworthy of our calling when we have multiple reasons to know we *are* worthy. If teachers feel helpless or even hopeless, demoralization is much more likely to occur when educators perceive that they lack support. Perhaps the final straw for many is to be evaluated on learning outcomes that are beyond their control. Marzano et al. (2001) estimated that what teachers actually control—instructional strategies, curriculum design (with Common Core mandates now), and classroom management—comprise only 13% of the variance in student performance. Yet they are now evaluated on 100% of the variance in student performance!

Perspective: Creative Teachers

Allowing and encouraging the innate creativity of teachers is a large part of recognizing their individuality. When we kill teacher creativity, we kill students' joy as well. As Odileke (2024) observes, we can fall into the trap of treating learning as just a means to an end, with the "end" being an annual standardized exam. The wonder and excitement of learning must emanate from inspired teachers in order to inspire students in a pedagogical process.

Many teachers have a "teachable moment" opportunity but balk because it throws off the schedule for the day. Some might have an idea for engagement that looks different from a posted lesson plan. The fear that it may reflect badly on them in a scheduled or nonscheduled walk-through evaluation gives them serious pause. Such fear and loss of creativity blunt the reason for choosing the profession of teaching for many. Why allow a system, we ask policymakers, that creates this stifling environment that kills teacher autonomy? Those who see education primarily as a science (or business) or those who know our schools only at the macro-level have convinced many educators that we have best practice now. We do not have best practice when we exclude the creative art of teaching. Why not recognize educators as women and men in the arena?

Perspective: Teachers in the Arena

Theodore (Teddy) Roosevelt was likely the most popular (besides Washington) and charismatic president the United States has had. He epitomized boundless energy as an adult after a sickly childhood. He busted up stifling monopolies, built the Panama Canal, preserved the existence and beauty of national parks, and enacted child labor laws. Teddy Roosevelt was a celebrated author, naturalist, and outdoorsman, and likely the most educated president of all. He had his flaws and faults like a certain wonder lust in leading a dangerous charge up San Juan Hill in the Spanish-American War. But, he had a firm belief in what was right, a certain magnanimity that led him to not seek another four-year term because he had already served almost seven years—due to President McKinley's assassination. He later regretted his decision to not run in 1908. In Paris in 1910 he gave his "legacy speech" which came to be known as "The Man in the Arena":

> It's not the critic who counts; not the man who points out how the strong man stumbles . . . The credit belongs to the man who is actually in the arena, whose face is marred by dust and sweat and blood; who strives valiantly; who errs, who comes up short again and again, because there is no effort without shortcoming . . . who at the worst, if he fails, at least fails while daring greatly, so that his place shall never be with those cold and timid souls who neither know victory nor defeat.

Teachers who yearn to transform are in the arena. Educators with strong identities strive valiantly. How we see teaching is a mindset just as is how we view our overall identities as educators. Before we approach "how" in teaching, which is where we seem to hover in the profession most of the time, it is vital that we do some professional self-examination.

As school leaders we would do well to seek clarity in our role as well. If our goal is for teachers to engage learners to spark achievement, leaders must commit to three simple objectives:

1. Center classroom environments on learners and learning. All other objectives will fall in place and be met if students are put first. Imagine if every school prioritized how students learn before how teachers teach.
2. Prioritize the hiring and development of transformational teachers because they center their teaching on their students. Make professional development about all three roles, not just one or two.
3. Make professional development (PD) about all three roles, not just one or two. PD on teaching to the whole learner with emphasis on the relater role surely wil stimulate lively interactions.

We are more than our intellectual/academic selves. There is a certain built-in wholeness or coherency in our brains. So why not encourage teachers to teach to our brain's potential?

Coherency in Securing Identity

Coherency in an academic process is a virtue lost as "jug to mug" pedagogy has ascended. Coherency in our teaching is not just about a certain logical consistency, which standardized teaching might boast, but about having a quality of a unified whole in curriculum and pedagogy. For example, when we experience something joyful like a new job offer or a new addition to the family, we should celebrate our emotion by writing down (briefly) our feelings that day and storing the notes away for rainy days that certainly will follow. The celebration involves "recognizing" coherency in ourselves.

Coherency as part of identity is emotional as well as logical. Narrowly defined teaching matched to academic achievement lacks coherency. The rise of informational teaching can be explained not just due to outside demands, but because it dovetails nicely with standardization's ascent, requiring less planning and less time than more student-centered processes. It meets the educational expediency-criterion.

Yet many teachers fervently desire to go beyond the expedient to do what they can to boost engagement and change lives. We have heard that learning is a process. So is teaching, and, for sake of comparison, it is definitely less complex than learning, just as transmitting is simpler than the act of receiving and comprehending. The best teachers are prepared to lead in their practitioner role.

Teaching is a coherent matter of being prepared to lay out the inspiration, the resources, and the structure for students in a learning environment. Strong identity in teaching can be observed and therefore analyzed more easily than learning, which often has facets that defy observation. But when teachers are observed, especially in the case of transformational teachers, they should be recognized for their individual expertise. The "system," especially in education, must not disregard its people, just as educators and students must not disrespect a system that allows independent and strong identities.

> ### Final Thoughts
>
> Teachers are as individual as their students. Teacher identity must be strong to cope with and succeed in today's "arena" of standardization. We must know who we are in order to assist our students become all they can be through transformational learning. Contemporary schools would have us permanently diminish and dwindle our spectrum of pedagogical opportunities down to coverage of core standards in preparation for tests that do little in assisting teachers in knowing their students diagnostically.
>
> Coverage of subject matter is one of the least effective teaching strategies, the most irrelevant, and the easiest way to teach, yet is all but mandated in standardized schooling. It has become a default role such as to affect teacher identity. Good teachers realize they are not bringing their best as they are pressured to cover standard after standard in their practitioner role. One of the significant reasons for low teacher morale in our U.S. public schools is because of unrecognized individual expertise.
>
> Other roles like developing critical thinking skills, inspiring learners, trusting teachers with curriculum choices, and encouraging students to learn independently form strong and relevant teacher identities. U.S. society would be well-served to finally recognize the value of supporting and developing not just the efficacy of students but also of their teachers. The system and its people, both integral to success in schooling, must do better in finding a healthy synergy.

10

Fostering Student-Centered Teaching

Myth # 10	*Fact # 10*
High-quality core standards produce more learning.	High standards are important but readiness to learn is essential. Foisting rigorous grade-level learning standards on students can frustrate learning. Developing "strategic learning qualities" in students promotes life-long learning.

As the familiar adage states, every journey begins with a first step. For educators it could not be more relevant: Teachers' attitudes and philosophy toward learning in their classroom is the beginning of their pedagogical journey. Do we proceed in our priorities thinking about standards for our subject, or do we reflect first on how our students can succeed? Standards are essential for good schooling because educators and students need their structure for guiding them toward higher expectations. Higher expectations lead to high levels of frustration, however, without teacher sensitivity to individual students' learning needs. To prioritize student learning, the concept of *readiness* is the vital counterbalance in successful classrooms. Without attention to readiness, standards become impotent and the goal of learning is lost. Standards are subject-centered, a good thing. Readiness is a student-centered reality, a better thing.

What is readiness as a concept in the educational world? It has many dimensions, but here is a concise definition: Readiness is the perceived balance between nature and nurture in a student's life. Nature is built into us; nurture pertains to the world of objects and others outside of us. Educators have a sacred responsibility to ascertain learners' readiness to learn, because without this care, students are impending casualties of dispirited frustration.

Perspective: Helping and Changing

At a university pinning ceremony recently a speaker described nursing as a helping-profession traditionally but suggested it is best described as a profession of changing lives. Teaching is a helping profession traditionally, but it too is more. Teachers can transform lives every day if that is their goal. When teachers walk through the school door each morning, what do they feel? Excitement about the day ahead in relating to students? Hopefully the emotion is more than "how can I help?" Or more than "I hope I can cover that whole set of standards today." Teachers have a privileged opportunity to transform learners as they begin each day. Mary Bethune was a pioneering U.S. educator over a century ago who believed that education is the key to breaking the cycle of poverty for African-Americans. She began with starting a literary and industrial school for disadvantaged girls. Later she founded Bethune-Cookman College which is now considered a model for Black colleges. She was asked to serve as an education and civil rights advisor to three presidents—Coolidge, Hoover, and FDR. She made a difference because she wanted to change lives.

All of us learn as affected by a unique maturation of our central nervous system and by the impact of our cognitive, emotional, and sensory experiences. How do we know when learners are ready to learn? We first center on them, not standards, observing how they are responding to the content being introduced. Simply, do they seem frustrated or bored? Or, perhaps it is not the content. Is there anxiety present?

> **Perspective: Not Herself Today**
>
> Sometimes readiness to learn is affected by anxiety coming from outside the classroom. Are we teachers sensitive enough to recognize it, and prepared to confront it? Frey et al. (2019) write of the idea of a "talking chair," an oversized chair where students know they can sit and share in class, between classes, at lunchtime, or even after school. The teachers don't pry but offer a sympathetic ear. Too often the process of "nurturing" goes awry outside the classroom.

Readiness is thus multi-dimensional. Readiness inside the classroom is the idea behind differentiated instruction, which confronts students' readiness to learn. Tomlinson (2000) identifies four classroom elements relevant to differentiated instruction: content, process, products, and the learning environment. Content can be differentiated according to reading levels and sensory mode (seeing, hearing, touching); process can range from interest centers to time on task; products are about allowing different expressions of learning (like writing or artistic expression); and learning environments can differ in allowance of individual, group work, and student movement.

It's About Time

Time is also a factor in readiness to learn if we believe that *all* students can learn, that for all students it is only a matter of time and experience. Let me elaborate on something from the Introduction of this book where I used the analogy of "dining in" and "taking out" to describe the phenomenon of change or transformation in learning. Throughout our lives we are exposed to teaching in a classroom that we may have fully grasped ("dining in") or may not have fully understood at the time. Maybe it was something like the "theory of relativity" in a physics class. Perhaps we connected to part of it, but not all of it, because of the way the teacher explained it according to our experience or level of development. Thus, "take-out" occurs.

> **Perspective: Dining In or Taking Out?**
>
> Perhaps months (or years) later we read or saw something that illuminated the theory for us in a different way. Maybe we were sitting in a college classroom, in a coffee shop, watching a movie, reading a book, surfing the internet,

or relaxing in an outdoor setting. Suddenly we find we understand the whole, not just the part. Some might call it a "Aha moment," but it is not a matter of memory but understanding. "Take-out" is a part of our coping with our readiness level. We either "eat" it all when it is first taught, or we bag it for consumption later on when we are "ready." What we teachers must avoid, however, is "food" (curriculum) so unsettling that all is rejected—brain science would term this a neurological downshift which can lead to blocking (a sense that "I will never get this"—it is the way I push away sushi when served to me!). Young students, for example, can block/downshift on elementary mathematics early on, leading to years of frustration with math concepts like common fractions or long division. Fractions, for example, are a whole new world of peering into the parts of a whole number—it is wise for teachers to use a lot of pie charts and other hands-on, concrete objects to teach the concept. The fact that we did not forget the "part" from the first teaching means we learned something then. But, the concept of readiness means that we were not ready then to learn the "whole" until later. Whether it was our "nature," which is our cognitive developmental level, or our "nurture," where we simply lacked experience, we weren't ready when the first teaching occurred. Sensitive teachers are needed, but knowledgeable ones are needed as well who can present curriculum in different ways.

Our school era with grade-level standards pushes teachers to push ahead, ready or not. This concept prioritizes the curriculum and the annual test, not the students. Often learning does not occur, and frustration settles in. Or, sometimes as posited above, learning in part occurs. Maybe the teacher failed as a practitioner, or maybe the concept was just too advanced for the student at the time. Or, perhaps the teacher was wise with intentionality to simply plant a seed that would grow later into full blossom. All of this "takeout" learning could be viewed as part of readiness to learn, demanding that teachers and schools always recognize who their learners are.

Perspective: Time and Space

Albert Einstein was known (Graydon, 2023) for his thought experiments. He had the remarkable ability to imagine practical scenarios interacting with complex scientific ideas like time and space. For example, he imagined passengers riding on a train throwing a ball back and forth, with a person outside at the station watching them go by through the train car window. The ball traveled at the same speed for all three even though the person at the station would perceive that the ball went much faster as it headed in the direction the train was traveling. Space and time (speed of light) are involved and both are equally relative. He would recall learning from past experience, turn it over in his mind, invent thought experiments, and apply his intuition to new conclusions, new learning. Einstein had a lot of takeout learning.

Schooling is very much something of a balancing exercise in pedagogy. Many educators have been forced into conformity, under rather irresistible pressure, to teach from a top-down standards-based platform. Students have not responded well as per state, national, and international testing over the last decade. On the other side of the balance beam, students need the guidance of wise and nurturing teachers in order to develop more bottom-up self-directed inquiry skills and knowledge.

Prioritizing Student-Centered Strategies

Much of the balancing that teachers must do hinges on the overwhelming factor of time. Teachers desperately want to promote transformational learning but seemingly cannot find the time because of standardized expectations. Given this time dilemma, let me make one of those "if-then" fanciful statements:

Perspective: Try, Try Again

If teachers can find the time to make only one "transformational" change in their pedagogy, then it must be the encouragement of more, actually much more trial-and-error learning. I say this because most of us perceive that the current standardized system by its nature of rigid accountability, builds in a great fear of failure among a whole generation of students (and teachers, too). We learn by succeeding *and* failing. It is another "divine and" in education. Our mistakes, not correct answeres, grow our intelligence. Failure in learning must become a relative term. Instead, the mindset of our students can become, "Try, try again." Students must be allowed to struggle and to err within a supportive classroom environment created by a transformational teacher. It is productive struggle that illuminates failure with enduring purpose in group discussions, case study analysis, writing assignments, presentations with peer feedback, and other constructive feedback activities. Time limits do dictate our use of direct instruction as is appropriate, but building in risk of error with intentionality is comparably invaluable.

Balance in pedagogy confronts students' readiness to learn. In Chapter 2, the place for exposition/lecture was highlighted and discussed. Here we can take the opportunity to analyze the left side and middle of the "Continuum of Teaching Strategies" where we find Inquiry and Discussion, respectively. To transform students we must meet them where they are, and focusing more on self-directed learning increases the likelihood. Guided Inquiry Teaching and Discussion strategies effectively foster self-directed learning.

Guided Inquiry Teaching

On the left side of the continuum is Inquiry. There have been various names given this method by educators. Krajcik and Shin (2014) are specific in calling for "project-based learning." I choose to call it *Guided Inquiry Teaching* because the term subsumes discovery learning, problems-based teaching, and project-based learning. And, insertion of the word "guided" brings an otherwise student-directed method under the guidance of teachers who must meet specific objectives.

Many want to disregard student-directed approaches because of (1) time issues, (2) clinging to the traditional teacher role, and (3) confusion over research showing inquiry/pure discovery methods as ineffective (Tuovinnen & Sweller, 1999; Kirschner et al., 2006). On this latter point, inquiry when left open to pure discovery might be fun for a while for learners, but without the structure of teacher-guidance this pedagogy is ill-advised and ineffective.

There is no doubt that teachers feel more time pressure than ever because of mandated year-end testing as well as various so-called "I-Ready" (or other) pre-exams throughout the year. Adding the perceived burden of guided inquiry teaching might seem counterintuitive to teachers. And, giving up the teacher role for a facilitator role demanded by inquiry takes belief, intentionality, suspension of some control, and patience that many teachers find unrealistic. Plus, they may be aware of or have experienced the extremes of teaching that was unfettered by structure and lacking purpose.

Indeed, some avoid more student-centered instruction because, by its nature, it is more relational, and that is too "messy" for some. It is ill-advised to sentimentally and mindlessly run toward student-centered instruction as a panacea because it is more socioemotional learning-oriented. But, *guided inquiry teaching works.* It is engaging to students and it is teacher-guided. The evidence is that teacher control and guidance are essential (Hattie, 2009) for the best achievement.

The biggest question to be answered about guided inquiry teaching involves time. Artitificial intelligence (AI) technology can assist. Dueck (2025) relates that ChatGPT can generate inquiry prompts connected to a standard. If we put student choice into the mix, that is, allowing each student or perhaps each group of students to choose their own prompt/topic. Then readiness is at least addressed if not satisfied. Dueck simply asks ChatGPT, for example, "Can I get 28 different prompts that would be appropriate for grade 9 students" (p. 16)? With AI, it is critical we ask a good question if we want a good answer. After tapping "enter," he received 28 different "avenues for learning." The use of AI in a time-compressed environment reduces the time needed in a part of the inquiry process where students/groups of students formulate specific topics to investigate. Below is a history inquiry lesson:

Perspective: Inquiry Learning

In *Transformational Teaching in the Information Age* (2011), we laid out a guided inquiry lesson on the American Civil War based on the driving question, "What was it like to live during the Civil War?" Students were asked to brainstorm using authentic Civil War family letters as a springboard from that historical period. Part of the teacher's role was to record responses, then categorize them into research topics like health, communication, transportation, education, battles in the war, family cultures, and more. Within these topics, AI could be used for generating more specific avenues of learning. Research is strong on the benefit of student choice. Students are allowed to *choose* (by listing first, second, third choices) which topic/prompt they wanted to research within groups. Google can assist with research. After presentations and exhibitions are made, a comprehensive assessment concludes the lesson. Contrast this learning process with what typically occurs in more teacher-centered pedagogies. Students can feel ownership of their learning. Teachers can meet standards and be goal-directed. And, there may be some enthusiastic learning in the classroom!

So, what matters to us in pedagogy? If we really want to engage students and enable deep understanding, we must allow learners to inquire under the guidance of expert teachers more often. Krajcik and Shin (2014) say it this way: "To form useable understanding, knowing and doing cannot be separated, but rather must be learned in a combined fashion that allows for problem-solving, decision-making, explaining real-world phenomena, and connecting new ideas" (p. 275).

If we truly desire to transform learners in our schools, guided inquiry teaching is a teaching strategy that surely leads to engagement because it:

1. Involves students deeply in the process,
2. Allows students to "own" their learning,
3. Permits teachers still to set and meet goals and objectives, and
4. Leads to valid evaluations of student learning.
5. Readily incorporates trial-and-error learning.

Student-directed instruction guided by a capable teacher has been shown to be strongly effective (Bransford et al., 2000). And, research (Boss, 2018) has demonstrated that students in project-based classrooms achieve more than students in traditional classrooms.

Some mistrust inquiry as a pedagogy: Even student-talk is now sometimes considered an ineffective pedagogy because it is not teacher-controlled, time-efficient, and goal-oriented enough. Time is a phalanx for standardized education and any perceived meandering from tightly controlled frameworks is dubious. Can we all take a deep breath?

No doubt that small-group discussion and inquiry are less teacher-dominated (the teacher's role changes to facilitator), but to be effective, any pedagogy, including exposition, must still involve planning for process and product. While I have said guided inquiry teaching cannot be a majority-of-the-time pedagogy in U.S. classrooms, it holds great promise when strategically planned and executed, especially because technology lends itself so easily as a research tool for this methodology. Process-goals can facilitate product-goals as we shall see. Good education always depends on what our desired ends are.

Small-Group Discussion

In the middle of the "Continuum of Teaching Strategies" is discussion. In his landmark book, *Visible Learning* (2009), John Hattie argues from his meta-analysis of 50,000 studies on achievement that great teachers are open to the best pedagogy needed to match their students' learning needs. That is, visible learning is a process of "eyeing" the effects teachers have on students. And, it is a process of students' being guided by teachers, based on diagnosed needs, on what to do and how to do it. By encouraging more student-talk and less teacher-talk, we have more opportunities to listen to our learners.

This of course is real evaluation. Thus, what is taught is learned when the process is visible (and audible) and explicit. Teaching and learning become one! Learning happens as we are teaching.

The process is one of mutual transformation. To see learning as the priority of teacher instruction is game-changing not only for teachers, but for learners who see their teachers as the key to their continued learning. A thesis in this book is that teaching and learning is transformational when the whole student is considered. Nothing but all is sufficient for transformational pedagogy.

Hattie argues that effective teachers are not shackled to specific methods but instead focus regularly on evaluating, monitoring, and then adjusting teaching methods accordingly. This speaks to an emphasis on process. The joy comes when we realize that we have arrived at a full destination of transformational learning while we were otherwise focusing on the journey. "Unguided" inquiry or the idea of pure discovery and student-guided learning is a nonstarter and unsupported by years of research, including Hattie's, as I have cited above. But, we must be careful to not jump to conclusions (sometimes called transductive thinking) based on that research about the value of small-group interaction.

The most rigorous and deepest learning takes place when we focus on the means not the ends, while still knowing where we are going (product); but, to get there we must focus intently on the proper steps (process). The process often involves using the scientific method of stating a problem, offering tentative solutions (hypotheses), researching the solutions (testing the hypotheses), and presenting findings (forming a conclusion).

Teacher–student and student–student interaction constitute the makeup of classroom discussion. Guided inquiry teaching relies greatly on small groups of students' researching and talking to each other under the guidance of their teacher. The teacher role does not change as being the adult in the room, focusing on individual student needs, structuring content according to standards and goals, leading interaction. But, teacher–student interaction in small groups can also utilize exposition.

Small-group discussion (and instruction) is often seen as a follow-up to whole group exposition to reinforce or reteach specific skills and concepts. Orlich et al. (2007) say,

> When implementing small-group discussions, you must decide on the proper amount of teacher control for the activity: You can dominate the activities of the groups almost totally, you can act in an egalitarian manner, or you can choose not to participate at all. Likewise, you must decide how much control you want the group leaders to exert within their groups.
>
> (p. 264)

Depending on the goal or purpose of small group discussion, the size of the group will range from four to six students. One overriding purpose of the group discussion, of course, is building and improving relationships. Students need time to talk with each other, and small groups can encourage communication, but they need guidance and oversight. Academic, social, and spiritual (personal development) goals can be met through the engaging and interactive experiences created in small group discussions. The teamwork skill so essential in this century is developed through peer-to-peer interactions. And, communication skills are developed through group presentation assignments.

Perspective: A New Kind of Listening

Frey et al. (2019) discuss ways to avoid isolated learning and poor engagement within small groups. An eighth grade humanities teacher used peer evaluations, shared publicly, of content and group presentation styles as a

> way to improve engagement. And, the teacher, Mr. Westbrook, introduced iterative presentations, where instead of assigning topics, the teacher gave a presentation and then asked a group to give a five-minute presentation on the teacher's presentation later that day or the next day. Mr. Westbrook said, "It realy prompts a new kind of listening, too, because a team doesn't know whether they will be selected until the end of the presentation" (p. 95).

Fostering small group dynamics in classrooms takes a commitment to planning time and follow-through. The by-product of using more self-directed learning strategies like discussion grouping and guided inquiry is the development of what we termed (Rosebrough & Leverett, 2011) "strategic learning qualities." To transform lives we must teach for learners' ownership of these qualities.

Strategic Learning Qualities

While rigorous core standards are designed to deepen knowledge, the process of teaching to them in a test-driven learning context has led to what amounts to coverage that is a mile wide and an inch deep. In order to confront both depth and wholeness in students' learning, teachers must create pedagogy that allows for the development of learning qualities that emanate from learning environments that are more student-centered and thus more learner-directed. Teacher instruction and time focused on the development of "Strategic Learning Qualities" (SLQs) are needed. When students are asked to work hard and solve problems in a more supportive environment, they acquire these SLQs and build a disposition toward life-long learning. We must teach so that our students know how to learn.

Ormrod (2012; 2019) notes that many students do not develop effective learning strategies on their own and need teachers' explicit instruction. She also cites research that newly acquired declarative (facts) knowledge and procedure (how to) knowledge require consolidation time, sometimes as much as hours and days or longer. For students it is being metacognitive because they do become aware of their own thinking over time that they possess these qualities.

Here are six SLQs (Rosebrough & Leverett, 2011):

- Curiosity—a quality that encourages learners to freely explore anything and everything. It is the trait that teachers must nurture passionately. Curiosity is a defining human quality.
- Openness—a quality that serves learners well in critical self-reflection on previous assumptions. Openness frees learners to discuss anything with others.
- Skepticism—an attitudinal quality that begins with openness and allows students to test and apply new perspectives through critical questioning. At its best, skepticism is a confident and humble search for the truth, especially in the face of dogmatism.
- Civility—a disposition that allows learners to display kindness and respect for others. It is a willingness to interact peacefully and to collaborate with students and teachers in a classroom.
- Persistence—an attitude tied to purpose. Learners persist with purpose despite obstacles. Teachers can encourage persistence by providing needed learning resources and appropriate emotional support.
- Imagination—a creative spirit that reaches beyond the senses (remember that creativity is not born from a vacuum of knowledge). This important quality takes learning from the objective to the subjective and back again. Albert Einstein said that "imagination is more important than knowledge" (Isaacson, 2007, p. 7).

These are not qualities that disappear in late spring of every year after a series of standardized tests. These qualities are like patient children on a long trip who take in the sights along the way and stop asking, "Are we there yet?" There is motivation and engagement because as travelers all students know learning is a journey not a destination. Transformational teachers also know it is not a race.

Costa and Kallick (2008) introduced 16 "Habits of Mind" in their book. They say that they require a certain cognitive consciousness and practice. I note that the six SLQs coincide with or bear similarity to seven of their "habits." Openness overlaps with both "Thinking flexibly" and "Remaining open to continuous learning." It is a process of development for our "qualities" or their "habits."

Similarly, Kallick and Zmuda (2017) say "when students are given the opportunity to pursue a project, they develop their "mind muscles" by creating, imagining, and innovating" (p. 11). SLQs are acquired by students when they are allowed to pursue and own their learning. Their learning happens along the way as a process. Learners must continue to practice the procedures of acquiring knowledge to improve their performance and to build SLQs. It is process-learning but importantly they acquire the product of SLQs as well.

For example, *imagination* is the result of learners' having a setting or learning environment that encourages thinking outside the senses. The most imaginative people in history were not necessarily traditionally "schooled," but they did find learning settings where they could develop their thinking. Walt Disney (who enjoyed art in school but eventually dropped out) and even Einstein (in Europe) found school to be tedious and dispiriting. Einstein would do thought experiments like riding on beam of light. Disney animated a mouse and built an empire of movies, television, and theme parks around the innovation.

We as educators realize that these qualities exist, regardless what we term them. Duckworth (McKibben, 2018) calls these qualities "intellectual character strengths." She says these strengths of mind "are kind of obvious, (and) schools could do a lot better job in developing them" (p. 42). I could not agree more. Students need schooling that gives SLQ-development opportunities to thrive.

One of the obvious ways to develop SLQs is through activities that encourage problem-solving. Any teaching method that extends thinking and intellectual curiosity, that encourages exploration of topics of particular interest, or allows struggling or advanced students to move toward greater depth are likely to develop SLQs. Problem-solving, which is a form of inquiry as a pedagogy, enables learners to use their knowledge and skills to confront new situations, effectively transferring previous learning (Ormrod, 2019). Do we teach so that our students are allowed *openness* to ideas?

Perspective: Open to All

Twentieth-century sculptor, Daniel Chester French, created the marble figure that sits brooding in the Lincoln Memorial. It was his unique task to be open to the idea of finding a way to present a mythic stone figure of Abraham Lincoln who was also recognizably a man. He gave America the most revered sculpture in our nation's capital. He took his first art lessons from May Alcott, the "Amy" of *Little Women*. Thus, he learned from a teacher! Somehow he was open to the fusion of the real with the ideal. He was also open to going against his instinct to create a standing Lincoln. He realized he needed a seated figure that was closer to eye-level, relative to the space. French sculpted the 16th president 19 feet high with 28 blocks of white marble and dedicated the iconic memorial in 1922. As French's biographer, Harold Holzer (2019), writes, he created "an enthroned hero gazing hypnotically at the national capital from a grand temple dedicated to the Union he had saved."

Are you a *skeptical* person? That is, have you developed the quality of questioning something that people all around seem to accept as fact? This quality looms especially large in today's world of social media and AI claims and pressures. Ostroff (2016) reminds us how Socrates encouraged his students to call everything into question. His method was unusual in that no definitive knowledge came from his teaching. His was a road to critical thinking empowered by skepticism.

If no other SLQs are learned, *civility* is the one essential. The Latin root word is "civilis," meaning a sense of relating to public life, of being a good citizen. Kindness and respect are embedded here. A transformational teacher's motto could be, "Education toward civility." Young learners must be taught to develop this quality in small groups—it does not come naturally with egocentric kindergarteners, for example. Older learners (including college students) must be reminded of what they hopefully learned in kindergarten. Civility shines even when we do not like someone very much. Teachers must monitor and demand and model kindness and respect in their classrooms.

How do we teach our students to *persist*? Focusing on the process rather than the outcome helps. Here's a simple analogy I have used with doctoral students in educational leadership as they begin their degree program.

Perspective: The Quality of Persistence

Earning a doctorate is unlike the process involved in any previous degree, often forcing a crisis of spirit and discouragement. It is a new process because the core of the degree is contributing new knowledge through writing a dissertation, challenging coursework, and consolidating focused knowledge into a review of literature. Steady steps have to be taken in a prescribed order and completed before taking the next step. I tell our new doctoral students to consider a simple metaphor that our task is to trim a long row of bushes growing in the front of a house. The killer of our efforts is to look ahead to see how much we have left to cut. That glance ahead can be discouraging! Instead, to stay in the moment of persistence, we keep our heads down, stay positive, focus on the present, but allow ourselves to occasionally gaze backwards to celebrate what we have accomplished in "clipped bushes." The outcome depends on a strategic process.

We make a big mistake in contemporary schooling with the overemphasis on outcomes. We need goals and outcomes to guide us and to become "accomplished" people, but life and education are found in the flow of doing rather than the feat of completing. It is about what we overcome. Not that there is anything wrong with finishing or mastery—it is greatly satisfying to look back with a sense of accomplishment, but learning is what happens along the way.

Curiosity allows us to freely explore everything as we learn. I noted in the Introduction that it was Csikszentmihalyi (Gardner et al., 2001) who famously described the psychology of *flow* as a mix of time and emotion. When we are able to become so curiously engaged in our task that we empower our emotional selves to conquer the bindings of time, we have accomplished flow in our learning process. It is a human moment or set of moments where we are lost in seemingly effortless performance. Persistence is here as well.

Perspective: Teacher Flow

Experienced teachers know flow. They know when they are in it—they never want it to end. Flow comes as a result of forethought and planning before a lesson, but is not guaranteed to happen. Students are caught up in the engagement of the moments of mesmerization (Csikszentmihalyi, 1997). They are learning and time is suspended—two coinciding occurrences that are rare. Flow pulls together and grips teacher, subject, and students academically, socially, and spiritually. Planning and expertise focus on academics. Sensitivity to guiding interactions arrests and maintains the social. And, intuitive insight into the emotions of individual students plumbs the depths of the spiritual. This is transformational learning.

Strategic learning qualities are developed, not taught directly. SLQs are learned as part of a process guided by a teacher who asks good questions and presents interesting problems to solve. Some of these qualities are developed through research work; some come from working with peers and interacting; some emanate imperceptibly because of a patient teacher; and some SLQs appear in stoked imaginations.

Core grade-level standards have a purpose: They are there to promote rigor which is not a bad thing in itself. However, we lose our balance when we deprioritize or ignore the students' readiness to learn within core standards. The concept of readiness is a psychology of balance in learning.

Ironically, attention to "Strategic Learning Qualities" as a goal for our students' learning can move us away from rigid standards, not from meeting them, but using them as our framework as we focus on more enduring qualities of learning in a healthy and transformational way. Setting the development of SLQs as a goal of instruction promotes more holistic process-oriented education, including more attention to learners' readiness to learn. More holism and focus on transforming student learning are antidotes for our lock-step tendencies in contemporary education.

Final Thoughts

Standards at their best are guard rails that enable teachers and learners to stay on course, like a car moving steadily ahead but slowing down or speeding up as necessary. Continuing with the analogy, the driver of the car is not

Mr. Standard, rather it is the teacher. Passengers are students being "driven" by an expert driver who stays on the road in a safe car (the school or classroom). The comparison is not perfect because, for one, the students in time need to drive their own cars, but the salient point is that standards should not be in the driver's seat such as they are in contemporary schools.

Enter the concept of readiness. If the driver is a set of core standards, the car's passengers will be unhappy, bored, frustrated, or afraid because the driver is incapable of pleasing them. The passengers (learners) are not ready for the inflexibility of the driver that is driving too fast, or too slow, or is simply not listening to them. Readiness is the human balance between nature (maturation of the central nervous system) and nurture (existing knowledge and experience) in every student. Challenging yet sensitive teachers are needed who know their learners well enough to transform their lives.

One of the most transforming concepts in education is teachers' mindsets to empower students to learn on their own and to want to continue learning for a lifetime. By focusing more on problem-solving and trial-and-error learning, transformational teachers can give their students the opportunity to develop "Strategic Learning Qualities" like curiosity, openness, skepticism, civility, perseverance, and imagination. The SLQs are part of a process of learning where students can inquire and research and choose under the guidance of wise teachers.

Conclusion

Any theory in any field of study is irrelevant if not aimed at practice. If teaching is the essential profession, our theory into practice (TIPS) must serve us well. We simply cannot allow the foundational treasure that is good educational theory and research to be ignored or replaced by those who are not only school-ignorant, but who do not have the best interests of our children in mind.

Educators often ask at least three questions, especially those serving in systems where standardization is smothering their creative impulses in teaching, "How do we push public schools to move away from putting too much emphasis on test scores?" "How do we bring about a change that focuses on prioritizing transformational teaching?" And, "How can we influence our peers, teachers that we work with every day, to improve or change their attitudes toward teaching?"

All three questions can be addressed with a similar response. The first question is a policy-level question, a macro-level query that is tinged with political dynamics. Teachers often feel powerless and small in systems that address the academic but either ignore or minimize social and spiritual goals. We see this when only academic outcomes are assessed and publicized.

We as educators, unfortunately, usually do not see the meaningful outcomes of our efforts to change lives. Teachers do not know the good they do because our students (1) are with us for only a short time, and (2) are like most humans who do not take the time to encourage others who are in their lives. Of all people, teachers must be reminded to persevere, that one person can change the world.

Perspective: Wilberforce

William Wilberforce was a British political figure who served Parliament in the late 18th and early 19th centuries. He thought at one point in his young life of serving people through the ministry, but was convinced by his mentor, John Newton (author of the classic hymn, "Amazing Grace"), and by other friends like William Pitt, the Prime Minister of the country at that time, that his character and oratory skills suited him well for a political era that needed great change. The slave trade was a particular scourge for Wilberforce's country which ruled the seas with a great fleet of ships. He worked in the House of Commons for five decades advocating for the abolishment of the slave trade, and then slavery itself in Britain. Wilberforce's efforts bore fruit and perhaps spared the United Kingdom a bloody civil war as was experienced a few decades after his death in the United States. One individual made a big difference.

U.S. education would benefit from a mighty shifting of power from those who know little about how children learn, policymakers, to those who know a lot, educators. While we impatiently monitor change in the political culture, we can influence change by modeling good teaching. Of course this shift requires an obligation by us teachers to know a lot about our subject and pedagogy. Teacher-scholars who prioritize the transformation of their learners will be engaged in a kind of subversive activity because of the contrast with standardized schooling.

Only the weight of best practice will begin to change the system. Parents must be educated in best practice. They must learn that optimal achievement can be realized through a pedagogical framework called transformational teaching because it affects the whole child, the whole adolescent, the whole learner. The research, as laid out in this writing, is overwhelming that knowledge, holism, inquiry, and interaction raise achievement. We can have it all!

Getting Real about Priorities

The second question about changing the focus within schools to prioritizing transformational teaching, and the third question about influencing peer attitudes toward teaching, are both micro-level in the classroom and best answered by educators who model the joy of transforming lives through education. Success breeds success in changing priorities and attitudes. This book has been about changing priorities and attitudes because we know that great teaching begins there. Kathyrn, an experienced teacher, points out some realities:

> How can teachers teach in the holistic way demanded by the Transformational Pedagogy Model? In theory, I know that we can successfully implement a more holistic method, but it seems that the current way our educational system is structured somewhat hinders our ability to emphasize a real transformation of the heart and head when we're so focused on teaching to tests. We are data rich, teaching poor, and all motivation is geared towards performance more than the joy of learning as it pertains to the reason why knowledge is valuable and to be desired.

She is poignantly accurate: Good theory in education does bring demands, not suggestions, because caring teachers want to do the right thing. Teachers are in an arena filled with critical powerbrokers sitting close up to courtside. Teachers are the players; the fans are more than fans, they are fanatics. Students are nowhere to be seen, except when we are making them into a ball to be tossed, kicked, or batted. This is a harsh metaphor but one that addresses an age-old question from harried teachers: "How can I possibly do this in this system I find myself in?" A different form of the same question is, "What do I do now? I love teaching my students and I don't want to quit on them." The answer has to be human in the most personal, not professional, way because in the end we must look within ourselves for courage and resilience. Mr. Rogers was right: The invisibles are essential. Overcoming enriches our lives more than achieving.

If we center blame on the system as the problem, we miss the solution. Indifference to best practices is where we must look, but also to the immeasurable realm we tend to ignore because of our human tendency to prioritize sensory input in our lives. How we view learners is crucial; they are more than we can readily perceive. In education, we need to embrace the self-discipline of synergizing academic, social, and spiritual goals. And, we must challenge ourselves to analyze and edify our strengths and weaknesses as scholars, practitioners, and relaters.

Teacher self-belief is crucial in such a time as this. But self-belief has to have a rock-solid knowledge foundation. What we believe about ourselves and our craft comes from what we know. Sometimes saying "I know" is even more transcendent than saying "I believe." As I have shared in this writing, we educators have had to deal with times of educational extremes before. "Data rich, teaching poor" is an appropriate phrase to describe the culture, realizing that none of us need to lecture good teachers because they are victims, along with students, of standardized crime. We can give teachers and students more than sympathy or empathy; we must give them support, part of which is undergirding knowledge. Knowledge is power.

Randall, a high school teacher, shares some frank words:

There was so much focus on testing and it is the topic of every conversation. I have witnessed some of the best educators that I have ever met being told they are failing at their job due to test scores. These were individuals who made sure they got to know their students and went beyond to make sure that their basic needs were met. The students loved them as they knew that they cared for them. It was unsettling to experience and I almost walked out of the education field entirely. I think the biggest thing that kept me going was the relationships I was building with the students in the classroom and on the field. The more time I got to know who the student was, the easier it became to teach the student. I have always tried to find ways to relate to every student I have had the opportunity to teach. I have found that in building these relationships my job as an educator has gotten a lot more rewarding. To me those relationships weigh far more significantly in contrast to test scores.

Caring for students of course is a starting point and must be combined with good scholarship and pedagogy. And, schools and school systems are not monolithic in their conformity to standardization's demands. Leadership in education, whether it is in the classroom, the building, or the district, is critical to the success of caring for learners.

Perspective: A Box of Chocolates

The whimsical line in the 1994 movie, "Forrest Gump," unfortunately, applies, "Life is like a box of chocolates, you never know what you're gonna get." The culture of the school is set by its leader, and the teachers and students are either the beneficiaries or the victims. Many teachers are astounded when they move from one county to another, in the same state, to find a warmer, more welcoming holistic educational environment. Such an experience demonstrates not only the power of priorities but also of transformational leadership.

In this book, I have proposed that we stamp *transformational teaching* as the name for a plethora of student-centered approaches in 21st-century education. Busy educators often get lost in their moment of time as they consider contemporary approaches to classroom instruction. Authentic learning, guided inquiry (problems-based learning), collaborative learning, and active learning are all quite student-centered at the conceptual level. Even interactive-lecturing is based on principles found more toward the center and left side of the "Continuum of Teaching Strategies" posted in Chapter 2. The extra oomph of an "attitude" of setting out to teach to transform, not just to inform, is needed to push all of these instructional approaches into the Transformational Pedagogy Model (TPM). No matter the system, no matter the arena, teachers can make a transformational difference that begins with an "oomph."

The contrast is stark in purpose for schooling. Purpose presupposes questions: What does success mean in schooling?

Why do teachers teach? What is a good teacher? What is a successful learner? A teacher (in 2025) says that "if my students are producing the data points approved by the district, I am a successful teacher. Something is fundamentally wrong with that." Teachers whose purpose is to transform, not just inform, are committed to meeting short- and long-term goals.

Time

We change lives when we teach critical skills and knowledge necessary for world-class academic education, *and* when we teach to lasting values in the social and spiritual realms like work ethic, tolerance, compassion, respect, responsibility, grit, and empathy. Academic knowledge is essential to a happy life, whether it is literature, mathematics, science, economics, or history. Social and spiritual development is also essential but in a different way because of its rather immeasurable nature.

Do we have to choose between the two goal structures as though it is academic versus social/spiritual? Of course not, most educators want both. And, in fact, a good academic education carries valuable character development with the development of strategic learning qualities (SLQs) (as found in Chapter 10). But standardized schooling has in essence said that we *do* have to choose because its commitment is to knowledge we can measure. Largely the dilemma is all about time.

Transformational learning has a *sacred* quality because it touches the timeless. Lock-step academic standards and informational teaching are more *secular* by contrast, if we view the word "secular" by its Latin root meaning, "time-bound." It is not necessarily a contrast concerning good versus evil.

Perspective: Clockwork

There exists no greater metaphor for the secular than a clock. Our most saliently human question is, "What do we do with the time we have?" Don't we want to fill it with the enduring as well as the immediate? Sacred and secular goals can be complementary if we do not gravitate to the extremes in our educational thinking. Standardization is an extreme form of traditional approaches to pedagogy, but teaching students without standards is also extreme. Lack of standards is not the problem currently: Teachers feel a tyranny of time as they cope with too many standards and lockstep expectations for them to teach to them. The consequence is a tragic shallowness in learning. Education and schooling have a timeless quality IF we strive to embrace it. The timeless quality is found in our students, not in academic goals, not in so-called teacher accountability where teachers cannot control most of the variables on which they are judged. Eternity is now and ongoing. Education has the power to transform learners for the present and the future.

Transformational learning occurs with teachers who have high expectations balanced with attitudes of integrity. It is time to change. Petrilli (2015) says that "nobody can say that teacher evaluation efforts are going well. This was an unforced error of enormous magnitude" (p. 1). More accountability for every living person or thing in education has not resulted in higher continual achievement for U.S. students. This statement is not meant to convey a lack of belief in strong results for schools, especially for disadvantaged students (where the gap is widening again). But high-stakes testing has ushered in an era where test scores have served as not only evidence of learning but learning itself.

This observation begs a question or two: If we are seeking joyful learning for our students, why is schooling not more focused on the "immeasurable," as for example the most important aspects of character? Again, *What is successful schooling?* Might there not be something wrong with the definition or conception of success in our schools? Even if educators focused on just one quality like gratitude, what a difference it could make! Grateful hearts make great people.

Perspective: Character Counts

Consider a literary example. Jean Valjean, a bitter French ex-prisoner in the Victor Hugo classic, *Les Misérables*, experienced a life transformation out of gratitude to a kindly bishop who forgave and refused to turn him over to the gendarmes concerning some purloined silver. Sometimes heartfelt gratitude comes after being forgiven (even when unmerited like Valjean), and sometimes gratitude comes in the aftermath of someone else's sacrifice. It deserves to be a spiritual goal in our schools.

Character traits can be more socially oriented like cooperation or a sense of responsibility. Social goals in the TPM have to do with social awareness, or learning ends that better human welfare. I separate the spiritual from the social to emphasize a point. Social goals can be spiritual if students can be challenged to become more fulfilled by doing for others. To be genuinely concerned about others is transcendent. Meeting spiritual goals is a large part of transformational learning because we seek to enhance personal fulfillment and self-awareness. The spiritual in every one of us is personal, individual, unique, and timeless. It is the stuff of transformational learning.

Who we are as teachers makes a difference in how our students are motivated to achieve in classrooms. Here is where we grasp the wisdom of Socrates' words about knowing ourselves—where we have to identify who we are as teachers before we proceed in a classroom. It seems easier to lose ourselves in our more impersonal, standardized schools. It is also more difficult to find holism in pedagogy. As stated early in the Introduction, *it takes a whole teacher to teach a whole child*. Whole-learner education's value is found in several manifestations where teachers:

- Love their students.
- Practice informed empathy.
- See the significance of human curiosity, trust, and honesty.
- Value trial-and-error learning in their classrooms.
- Engage their community to come in and learners to go out.
- Learn about their students and chart courses of improvement from evaluations.

Mythologies and Facts in Education

Great teachers have always known that students come first, but even great teachers fall prey to misleading notions and unrelenting pressures in school environments. There is a great deal of evidence that U.S. public schools, with some exceptions, have lost their way. Scores are tragically low; teachers are leaving their jobs in record numbers; teacher morale has plummeted; students increasingly are exhibiting emotional trauma; relatedly, student absenteeism is peaking; states are pushing "grow your own" teacher apprenticeships due to record-low college teacher-preparation enrollment. The joy of schooling is gone missing.

A thesis of this book is to recover the lost joy of transformational learning in our schools and classrooms. It is lost because we have allowed a repressively standardized school culture to take root, one where some of the best pedagogical ideas of the past have been codified and calcified like exposition, structure, learning goals, and accountability. We can find the joy of transformational learning for our students, but we must undertake a search not unlike the Greek character, Diogenes, who (rather cynically) walked around Athens searching for an honest man with his lantern. His search was that of a philosophic cynic. Ours is one of practical exasperation. He was looking for honesty; we are looking for integrity in teaching in the midst of some engrained myths of pedagogy.

We teach for learners, not only to meet their academic needs but to transform their lives. Transformational teachers are know-ers, do-ers, and inspirers. By challenging the myths of teaching (our lever) we can discover how to make learning more transformational. The fulcrum for the lever of analysis of the myths has been the TPM which is based on educational research and best practice.

Sometimes in concluding we should summarize. Good teachers preview but also review. I want to review here but I also want to respond concisely to each myth of teaching I have challenged in this book. After graduate school I realized that, simply, it is not enough to state what you disagree with or think is wrong in the field of education. I must also take a stand on what I think and feel and know is right and better and workable, as I have attempted to do throughout this writing, as I recommend a framework called transformational teaching and learning.

Transformational Learning

The ten myths of pedagogy discussed in depth with ten accompanying chapters can be summarized with some theory into practice ways (TIPS) teachers can ensure transformational learning occurs in their classrooms.

Myth 1: Low expectations for student attention to our teaching are justified.

If we aim low, we will miss the target. Research has shown that high expectations lead to engagement and higher achievement if we place inspiration before information. Curiosity is there in our students if we inspire and connect by using the full spectrum of pedagogies. In the 21st century, teachers are competing against accessible and personalized technologies for the attention of their learners, unlike any generation before. Attempts to pound in information will indeed lead to bovine eyes and blank stares. Trial-and-error problem-solving is a reasonable solution even with standardized time constraints, but teachers must walk alongside their students as relaters because errors and mistakes engender fear. Transformational teachers can deliver learners from their fears. Some TIPS:

1. Listen more carefully to what students ask and say. Learners at all levels want to be heard and respected. Our tendency as teachers is to plan more for our "asking and saying" than for what our students might convey.
2. Encourage more trial-and-error learning activities. When "controlled floundering" is allowed, teachers can engage students' curiosity. A caveat here is that trial-and-error learning, while stimulating, can also engender fear of failure. Transformational teachers have the empathy to recognize the fear factor and to allow learners to trust them.

Myth 2: Lectures do not work and kill enthusiasm.

Standardized schooling advocates should be thankful that this is a myth because the system currently demands a lot of exposition-based pedagogy. While great lecturers are few, exposition especially in the form of interactive lecturing can be highly effective, with the caveat of using it with a variety of other more student-centered pedagogies. The key to interactive lectures is avoiding the pedantic and instead connecting to the emotions and experience of the students. Research shows that by proceeding whole to part instead of the traditional analytic approach makes for more effective teaching. It is an enduring pedagogical principle that the brain learns when teachers build upon what students already know. How do we know what they know? We can look at the myriad of tests they have taken and diagnose, and we can ask questions and pay more attention to our students' comments and questions. Some TIPS:

1. Great lectures connect to our emotions; thus, it is vital to avoid "dry" exposition. A sure-fire way to connect is to include stories and anecdotes that are of human interest. For example, in a lecture lesson about the U.S. civil rights movement, do our students know that Michael King, the father of Michael Jr., on a trip to Germany in the mid-1930s was so inspired by Reformationist Martin Luther's memorial that he renamed his son (after renaming himself) Martin Luther King, Jr.?
2. The most effective teaching occurs when we lecture from whole to part as in beginning with the synthesis of the big picture. If our job is to introduce the operation of multiplication to third-graders, begin by telling and showing them that multiplication is a shortcut for addition. Two principles of pedagogy are involved here: First, most students learn more effectively when teachers proceed from general to specific; and, second, a brain-compatible principle is that our brains learn by building upon what we already know (in this case, addition).

Myth 3: More time on task means more effective teaching.

Time on task is an unreliable variable. How we view students is the beginning of transformational learning, which speaks to the quality of the teacher–student relationship. The process involved in engaging students in learning can hinge on the quality of questions and discussion in the learning environment. Less can be more if teachers stop and "posthole" curriculum. Teachers must be experts in using questions. Psychological flow in discussions is an optimal objective which can be achieved by taking steps to increase student ownership of their learning. The simple first step is allowing students more choice in what they study. Some TIPS:

1. In U.S. schools, the screws of accountability are tightened to demand more time on task with core standards, seemingly leaving teachers little time for creativity and thus transformational learning opportunities. One answer is for teachers to focus on enhancing the learning environment with a stronger focus on Bloom's ascending complexity of questions and more awareness of where discussions are headed. We can start any discussion with knowledge and comprehension-level questions, like "where did Christopher Columbus actually land on his voyage of discovery?" or "how many ships did he use and what were their names?" A question at a higher level is "what were Columbus' motives in taking such a dangerous trip?" Or, "what were the fears of the Spanish explorers as they proceeded west across the Atlantic Ocean (they literally feared falling off the edge of the world as they knew it)?" When we place good question strategies into the center of our pedagogical focus, we maximize time and increase the quality of the class environment.
2. Another way to enhance the learning environment and to reduce the stress of meeting standard after standard is to focus on the psychological concept of "flow." We can allow students to own their learning and to be completely into what they are doing and saying. To achieve flow more often we first teach to inspire (show them a video of a Space X rocket in a perfect descent into the arms of a landing platform) and to allow them to inquire in small groups on questions of relevance to their lives, like "Is it feasible we will have humans on Mars in the next five years?" Flow involves "inner clarity" which is knowing what needs to be done, and how well it is done. Allowing students ownership of questions and learning-projects lowers the stress of the tedium of marching from one standard to another.

Myth 4: Teaching is a process of adding knowledge to a learner's cognitive storehouse.

This is a sad misperception of how we learn and how our brains operate. Our brains are electrochemical factories attuned to the social-emotional aspects of life. We remember what we feel. The evidence is overwhelming. What does this mean for teachers? It may be more important how learners feel in classrooms than how they perform. Research is very strong on the positive impact of caring teachers on students' achievement. We can have both the cognitive and affective. Some TIPS:

1. One way of connecting our teaching to how the brain functions is to seek to create a perception of physical objects and social aspects that seems new to learners. Virtually any kind of service-learning project fills the bill. One idea is to engage students in transforming the appearance of a neglected school exterior. Clearing weeds, tilling, and planting is not only a practical lesson in problem-solving, but the group work of environmental stewardship is novel and fulfilling.
2. The discipline of memorizing poems and other literature is accomplished through repetition and meaning. The great 19th-century U.S. poet, Henry Wadsworth Longfellow, wrote poems that had rhyme and rhythm and historical meaning, fertile ground for memorization. The American Revolution comes to life with "Paul Revere's Ride," a must for any fifth- or eighth-grade history or language arts class. The poem, "I Heard the Bells on Christmas Day," written from the timeframe of the American Civil War, is poignant and biographical in Longfellow's life. Young students have unique brains built to memorize and the time is worth it in the context of life-long learning.

Myth 5: Tests show what students have learned.

Tests are an important part of schooling because they can have a forward and backward effect. Forward effect is accountability—students need motivation to do their best. "Is this on the test?" is a significant question. "Of course it is," is a significant answer. The backward effect of testing is diagnosis of learning problems—assessment makes student learning visible to teachers, and it shows teachers how they as teachers are doing. The real test for learning is when we ask students to apply it in a different context outside the classroom—this is an assessment, too, and it is quite visible. Authentic learning tasks are to be prized because students are applying their learning on work they know is real. Some TIPS:

1. Tests should be for diagnostic purposes not indicative ones. Teachers can monitor and adjust their teaching based on standardized assessments as well as teacher-tests. If the diagnosis shows that a student lacks a basic understanding of common fractions, instruction for that learner must shore up this hierarchical math component, not move on to the next standard or focus only on the macro-indicative results. Hattie (2015) terms it "visible learning" which is the primary purpose of assessments: they give us learning made visible, calling for adjustments in our teaching. We have not taught until someone learns.
2. Authentic learning is learning directly connected to life outside the classroom, which is why internship and apprenticeships are so effective. At the high school level, teachers can bring in a local gourmet coffee shop manager to explain coffee beans, roasting, grinding, and brewing, followed by a field trip to the shop. The experience can be meaningfully tied to standards.

Myth 6: The best teachers are ones with reputations for rigor.

Transformational teachers challenge their learners but they are also sensitive enough to provide students with hope of succeeding. Unbridled rigor in teaching is harmful. Teacher-scholars are to be treasured, especially when they allow students to "fail" within an encouraging and supportive environment. Research shows a strong relationship between hope in the learning environment and achievement. Being hopeful is the opposite of being depressed. Some TIPS:

1. The act of writing down our thoughts, then refining them through more coherent drafts is a challenging experience. Journaling is a good starting point; polishing a paper represents proof of learning by trial-and-error application. While both are important, writing well is more difficult than speaking well, and perhaps more cognitively rewarding.
2. We inspire hope in learners by being sensitive to them in the face of frustration. Challenges inevitably produce frustrations, but teachers who take the time to look and listen change lives. School must be about success and transformational teachers give students hope by making sure they are ultimately successful in their work.

Myth 7: Fun teachers do not meet standards.

The process that is teaching begins with a caring knowledge of our students. We can insert joy into the classroom by choosing methodology that connects with emotions, like reading stories, using authentic learning, leading the students in outdoor activities, and helping learners exercise ownership in learning. Caring can breed competence if the challenge is appropriate and not a frustration. Students who experience both caring and challenge consistently achieve more. Group work can optimize choice and interaction among learners, which can make learning fun. Some TIPS:

1. Joy comes to us in many forms. The distractions of life like the stress of running late to catch a bus or plane, doing a home financial budget with limited funds, a child trying to sit still and quiet for too long, can be tempered by the escapes of music, laughter, physical activity, poetry, and more.
2. Allow students to "own their learning" by giving them problems to solve. The problems chosen for them or that they choose for themselves must be a challenge, not a frustration. Individuals can confront problems but so can groups. Teachers play a guiding role and allow the process to play out, whether it is a rubric cube or physics

question, like "which hits the ground first when dropped from a height of ten feet, a tennis ball or bowling ball?"

Myth 8: Technology can replace teachers.

Teachers have the opportunity to create pedagogical relationships with students, something that technology can never replace. A key understanding is that technology can assist by saving teachers a precious commodity in standardized schools: time. Having more time means teachers can embrace human interaction to build agency in learners. Teachers who build attitudinal qualities like realness, empathy, and prizing discover that they affect students' lives positively in a myriad of ways, including sharing a moral burden with parents and guardians for those being taught. A trust relationship undergirds transformational teaching and learning. Some TIPS:

1. Technology by definition assists teachers and students but is no substitute for caring relationships in a classroom environment. Transformational teachers can foster better relationships with learners by being real, being empathetic, and by making an effort to prize individual students. Many examples are detailed in Chapter 8.
2. Research is strong on the academic impact of warm and caring teacher-relater behavior. It should not be trivialized as a symptom of weakness in educators. Research also suggests that departmentalization (rather than self-contained classrooms) in the primary grades is not only ineffective with achievement but potentially harmful with student agency.

Myth 9: Coverage is a vital role for teachers.

A teacher's identity must be strong to foster transformational learning. Teacher identity includes personal values, professional values, and individual shaping from cultural experiences.

Teaching for coverage of a set of standards is a role imposed by standardized schooling, a vast waste of time. Teacher morale has been adversely affected because they have lost confidence in their calling to make a difference. Teachers need balance in their personal and professional lives for high teacher-efficacy, and they deserve recognition for transforming lives. Teacher-journaling can help to reset balance. Some TIPS:

1. Teacher morale in the United States is very low for multiple reasons. Standardized education's lean toward teaching for coverage must be resisted. One way toward stronger teacher-identity is for teachers to develop a mantra of "what I believe makes a difference." Teachers can believe, for example, that seeking depth in academics is an effective mindset. WIBMAD on a bracelet is a great reminder.
2. Coherency in teaching means we hold things together with meaning. We can combat the coverage-syndrome by choosing to "posthole" a topic now and again. If the Enlightenment is the topic, as an example, perhaps dig into the friendship between Scottish philosopher, David Hume, and American icon, Benjamin Franklin.

Myth 10: High standards produce more learning.

Raising standards is not a panacea for raising test scores. Moving from standard to standard in a test-driven culture does not prioritize or improve student learning because it ignores readiness to learn. Not considering learners' readiness to learn produces failure. Readiness involves a balance between nature and nurture as students confront any given task. Teachers can confront why they are teaching and what school is for. Ask, "What will my students be like when they leave my classroom, when they leave this school?" If the goal is to encourage life-long learning as an ethic and foster habits that make students better people, then pedagogy must center more on independent learning. Teachers with high expectations can assist in the development of SLQs "Strategic Learning Qualities" in learners like curiosity, openness, skepticism, civility, perseverance, and imagination. Pedagogy like discussion and inquiry (on the left side of the Continuum of Teaching Strategies) promotes SLQs that are the hallmark of independent learners. Some TIPS:

1. With the push to meet standards, students' readiness to learn can be a lost endeavor. Teachers can simply recognize that some learning will be "take-out" instead of "dining in" for students. Intentional "circling back" to vital concepts should be a common practice in monitoring learning.
2. Strategic Learning Qualities such as skepticism are developed by allowing students to question and to own their answers. Another SLQ is persistence. How do we teach our students to persist? Focusing on process rather than outcomes helps. John Wooden, legendary basketball coach at UCLA, taught his players about a pyramid of success, that winning games was simply (yet profoundly) an outcome of persisting and building through the details of the process: like how players lace their shoes, what kind of socks they wear, fundamentals like short passes on fast breaks, the mechanics of defending a player on the baseline. It is an attitude tied to purpose that overcomes obstacles.

Before Concluding

In this book, I have offered a challenge to the myths of teaching. The challenge is anchored by best practices on a foundation of seminal and current theory and research, not on Jerome Bruner's *folk pedagogy* (1996), which he says is a set of assumptions based on *intuitive* theories by laypersons and educators. He called them myths, half-truths, and convenient fiction. But, Bruner asserted that we should build upon these intuitive theories, not reject them outright.

Perhaps we should consider intuition for a moment. Good teachers are good leaders and the best leaders are strongly intuitive, relying upon a sense of what is right and good. Hunter Lewis (1990) provided a uniquely helpful definition of intuition as one of six ways we make personal choices in our lives (the other five: authority, sense experience, logic, emotion, and science). He says that intuition is "a highly developed and powerful mode of purely abstract thinking, one that synthesizes masses of facts and theories with extraordinary speed" (p. 52). Notice that intuition is not emotional in conception. Also, Lewis says that intuition is part of the unconscious mind which he asserts is immensely more powerful than the conscious mind.

Perspective: Growing Up

In a reflection on his childhood and adolescent years, Microsoft guru, Bill Gates (2025), says that if he were growing up today, he might be diagnosed on the autism spectrum as "neurodivergent." His parents "had no guidepost or textbooks to help them grasp why their son became so obsessed with certain projects, missed social cues and could be rude and inappropriate without seeming to notice his effect on others" (p. 15). Gates marvels that his parents were able to manage a precise blend of support and pressure for his needs, allowing room for emotional growth and opportunities for social skill development with peers, with groups like Cub Scouts and baseball teams, and with adult friends of his parents, "which fed my curiosity about the world beyond school."

Gate's parents had a strongly intuitive ability to manage parenting, by Hunter Lewis' definition. They made choices of support and challenge without texts and guides. It seems they had well-chosen standards to meet, allowing their son to grow up with a balance of parenting approaches that fit their son. Here we see balance.

Teachers are *in loco parentis* every day of school. It does not mean that we are parents at school because they are two different roles. But as we serve in the place of parents we cannot be successful in transforming lives without being uniquely in tune with our students, much like Gate's parents. The whole learner was nurtured and challenged and allowed to grow to potential, ironically without the technology we enjoy today.

Concluding

I began this book by asserting that the pedagogical framework called *Transformational Teaching and Learning* is a 21st-century model of student-centered research, theory, and practice worthy of adoption in U.S. schools. Teaching to transform can produce a joy in learning that can only fully come after a night of generational sorrow in the lives of our students and educators in contemporary U.S. public schools—to paraphrase a psalmist. William Butler Yeats wrote, "But joy is wisdom, time an endless song." As educators we can equate wisdom with joy if we follow the research in education and psychology. It is all there: curiosity, balanced pedagogy, good question strategies, brain-based teaching, smart use of tests, sensitivity to challenge and hope for learners, teaching to social-emotional learning, cultivating relationships in the classroom, nurturing teacher identity, recognizing readiness in learners, and teaching to develop SLQs in students. The power of education can transform lives if we seek balance in teaching to mind, body, and spirit. High morale and happiness will flow; good results will follow.

William Blake penned, "And I wrote my happy songs, Every child may joy to hear." Through our efforts with best practice we can write happy songs as someday pacing guides will be no more. And every child will be glad to hear the news.

References

Abeles, V. (2016, January). Is the drive for success making our children sick? *New York Times*. Retrieved from https://www.nytimes.com/2016/01/03/opinion/sunday/is-the-drive-for-success-making-our-children-sick.html?cubz=1

Abercrombie, H. C., Kalin, N. H., Thurow, M. E., Rosenkranz, M. A., & Davidson, R. J. (2003). Cortisol variation to humans affects memory for emotionally laden and neutral information. *Behavioral Neuroscience, 117*(3), 505–516.

Alderman, M. K. (2004). *Motivation for achievement: Possibilities for teaching and learning.* (2nd ed.). New York: Routledge.

American Psychological Association (2014, February). American Psychological Association survey shows teen stress rivals that of adults. Retrieved from https://www.apa.org/news/press/release/2014/02/teem-stress/aspx

Armbruster, P., Patel, M., Johnson, E., & Weiss, M. (2009). Active learning and student-centered pedagogy improve student attitudes and performance in introductory biology. *CBE Life Sciences Education, 8*, 203–213.

Armstrong, N., Chang, S. M., & Brickman, M. (2007). Cooperative learning in industrial-sized biology classes. *CBE Life Sciences Education, 6*, 163–171.

Armstrong, T. (2019). *Mindfulness in the classroom: Strategies for promoting concentration, compassion, and calm.* Alexandria, VA: ASCD.

ASCD + ISTE (2024). *Principles of transformational learning.* Alexandria, VA: ASCD.

Babyak, M. A., Snyder, C. R., & Yoshinobu, L. (1993). Psychometric properties of the Hope Scale: A confirmatory factor analysis. *Journal of Research in Personality, 27*(2), 154–169.

Bandura, A. (1986). *Social foundations of thought and action: A social cognitive theory.* New York: Prentice Hall.

Bandura, A. (2006). Toward a psychology of human agency. *Perspectives on Psychological Science, 1*, 164–180.

Barshay, J. (2018, May). Two studies point to power of teacher-student relationship. *Hechinger Report*.

Barshay, J. (2023, December). There is a worldwide problem in math and it's not just the pandemic. *Hechinger Report*.

Berliner, D. C. (2011). Rational responses to high stakes testing: The case of curriculum narrowing and the harm that follows. *Cambridge Journal of Education, 41*(3), 287–302.

Berliner, D. C. (2018). Between Scylla and Charybdis: Reflections on and problems associated with evaluation of teachers in an era of metrification. *Education Policy Analysis Archives, 26*(54), 3–23. Retrieved July 2019 from https://epaa.asu.edu/ojs/article/view/3820

Bloom, B. S. (1956). *Taxonomy of educational objectives, handbook: The cognitive domain*. New York: David McKay.

Blumenfeld, P., Kempler, T., & Krajcik, J. (2006). Motivation and cognitive engagement in learning environments. In R. K. Sawyer (Ed.), *The Cambridge handbook of learning sciences* (pp. 475–488). New York: Cambridge University Press.

Boss, S. (2018) With Larmer, J. *Project-based teaching: How to create rigorous and engaging learning experiences*. Alexandria, VA: ASCD.

Bransford, J., Brown, A., & Cocking, R. (Eds.). (2000). *How people learn: Brain, mind, experience, and school*. Washington, DC: National Academy Press.

Brown, L. (2025, March). Majority of teachers consider leaving profession, according to Mizzou study. *West Newsmagazine*. Retrieved from https://westnewsmagazine.com

Broyles, N. (2018, October). Learning character from characters. *Educational Leadership, 76*(2), 71–74.

Bruner, J. (1960). *The process of education*. Cambridge, MA: Harvard University Press.

Bruner, J. (1996). *The culture of education*. Cambridge, MA: Harvard University Press.

Bruning, R. H., Schraw, G. J., & Norby, M. M. (2011). *Cognitive psychology and instruction*. (5th ed.). Upper Saddle River, NJ: Pearson.

Bryan, C. (2025, February). Seattle schools see mixed results with digital math. Retrieved from https://www.seattletimes.com/education-lab/seattle/schools/see/mixed/results

Burns, M. (2024). Teaching smarter with AI. *ASCD Blog*. Retrieved from https://www.ascd.org/blogs/teaching-smarter-with-ai

Cariss, T., & Sullivan, T. (2019, July). Leverage data to close achievement gaps. *Voice of the Educator in MiddleWeb SmartBrief.* Retrieved from Https://www.smartbrief.com/original/2019/07/leverage-dat-close-achievement-gaps?utm-source-brief

Carvalho, P. F., McLaughlin, E. A., & Koedinger, K. R. (2017). Is there an explicit learning bias? Students' beliefs, behaviors and learning outcomes. In G. Gunzelmann, A. Howes, T. Tenbrink, & E. Davelaar (Eds.), *Proceedings of the 39th annual conference of the cognitive science society* (pp. 204–209). Pittsburg, PA: Cognitive Science Society.

Center for Disease Control (CDC). (2025, February). Data and statistics on children's mental health. Retrieved from https://www.cdc.gov

Collins, J. (2001). *Good to great: Why some companies make the leap... and others don't.* New York: Harper.

Costa, A. (1991). *Developing minds: A resource book for teaching thinking.* Alexandria, VA: ASCD.

Costa, A. L., & Kallick, B. (2008). *Habits of mind: 16 Essential characteristics for success.* Alexandria, VA: ASCD.

Cottingham, C. (2024, December). Integrating grammar and creative writing lessons. Retrieved from https://www.edutopia.org/article/integrating-grammar-creative-writing

Cove, K. M. (2025, January). Teaching strategies: How to make one-on-one ELA conferences work. Retrieved from https://www.edutopia.org/article/individual-student-conferences-class

Cranton, P. (2002). Teaching for transformation. *New Directions for Adult and Continuing Education, 93,* 63–71.

Csikszentmihalyi, M. (1997). *Finding flow: The psychology of engagement with everyday life.* New York: Basic Books.

Dahlgren, D. J., Wille, D. E., Finkel, D. G., & Burger, T. (2005). Do active learning techniques enhance learning and increase persistence of first-year psychology students? *Journal of the First-Year Experience & Students in Transition, 17,* 49–65.

Davis, H. A. (2003). Conceptualizing the role and influence of student-teacher relationships on children's social and cognitive development. *Educational Psychologist, 38*(4), 207–234. https://doi.org/10.1207/S15326985EP3804_2

Debaryshe, B. D. (2008). Joint picture-book reading correlates of early oral language skill. *Journal of Child Language, 20*(2), 455–461.

Deslauriers, L., Schelew, E., & Wieman, C. (2011). Improved learning in a large-enrollment physics class. *Science, 332,* 862–864.

Dewey, J. (1938). *Experience and education.* New York: McMillan.

Diliberti, M. K., Schwartz, H. L., Doan, S., Shapiro, A., Rainey, L. R., & Lake, R. J. (2024, April). Using artificial intelligence tools in K-12 classrooms. *RAND.* Retrieved from https://www.rand.org/pubs.research_reports/RRA95621.html.

Duarte, F. (2023, November). Average screen time for teens. *Exploding Topics.* Retrieved from https://exploding topics.com

Duckworth, A. (2016). *Grit: The power of passion and perseverance.* New York: Scribner.

Dueck, M. (2025, February). How to unpack a learning standard using ChatGPT. *Educational Leadership.* Vol. 82, No. 5. https://ascd.org

Durlack, J. A., Weissberg, R. P., Dymnicki, A. B., Taylor, R. D., & Schellinger, K. B. (2011). The impact of enhancing students' social and emotional learning: A meta-analysis of school-based universal interventions. *Child Development, 82*(1), 405–432. https://doi.org/10.1111/j.1467-8624.2010.01564.x

Dweck, C. S. (2007). *Mindset: The new psychology of success—how we can fulfill our potential.* New York: Ballantine Books.

Dweck, C. S. (2017). *Mindset: The new psychology of success.* (Updated ed.). New York: Random House.

Egyed, C. J., & Short, R. J. (2006, October). Teacher self-efficacy, burnout, experience and decision to refer a disruptive student. *School Psychology International, 27*(4), pp. 387–404.

Ende, F. (2019, February). So, what's up with personalized learning? Retrieved April 2019 from https://www.highered@smartbrief.com

Ferlazzo, L. (2019, November). Fair is not equal. *Education Week,* Retrieved https://www.edweek.org

Flint Journal (2025, January). Veteran teachers in a shared journey. Retrieved from https://www.mlive.com/news/flint/2024/12/meet-the-teachers-grand-blanc-educators-celebrate-32-years-of-teaching-together.html

Freeman, S., O'Connor, E., Parks, J. W., Cunningham, M., Hurley, D., Haak, D., Dirks, C., & Wenderoth, M. P. (2007). Prescribed active learning increases learning in introductory biology. *CBE Life Science Education, 6,* 132–139.

Frey, N., Fisher, D., & Smith, D. (2019). *All learning is social and emotional: Helping students develop essential skills for the classroom and beyond.* Alexandria, VA: ASCD.

Furrer, C., & Skinner, E. (2003). Sense of relatedness as a factor in children's academic engagement and performance. *Journal of Educational Psychology, 95*(1), 148–162. https://doi.org/10.1037/0022-0663.95.1.148

Gardner, H. (1999). *Intelligence reframed: Multiple intelligences for the 21st century.* New York: Basic Books.

Gardner, H., Csikszentmihalyi, M., & Damon, W. (2001). *Good work: When excellence and ethics meet.* New York: Basic Books.

Gates, B. (2025, January). Bill Gates: I coded while I hiked as a teenager. Was I on the spectrum? Probably. *Wall Street Journal.* Retrieved at https://www.wsj.com

Gazzaniga, M. (2001). Brain and conscience experience. In Cacioppo, J., Berntson, G., Adolphs, R., Carter, C., Davidson, R., McClintock, M., McEwen, B., Meaney, M. Schacter, D.. Sternberg, E., Suomi, S. & Taylor, S. (Eds.), *Foundations in social neuroscience* (pp. 203–214). Cambridge, MA: MIT Press.

Gee, K. (2019, March). *Co-founder of teen that app sees "loneliness epidemic" on the horizon.* New York: Wall Street Journal.

Gershenson, S., Hart, C., Hyman, J., & Papageorge, N. (2021, February). The long-run impacts of same-race teachers. *National Bureau of Economic Research.* Retrieved from https://www.nber.org.

Godwin, K. E., Seltman, H., Almeda, M., Skerbetz, M. D., Kai, Sh., Baker, R. S., & Fisher, A. V. (2021). The elusive relationship between time on-task and learning; not simply an issue of measurement. *Educational Psychology, 41*(4), 502–519. https://doi.org/10.1080/01443410.2021.1894324

Goodlad, J. I., Soder, R., & Sirotnik, K. A. (Eds.). (1993). *The moral dimensions of teaching.* San Francisco, CA: Jossey-Bass.

Gordon, G., with Crabtree, S. (2006). *Building engaged schools: Getting the most out of America's classrooms.* Princeton, NJ: Gallup Press.

Graydon, S. (2023). *Einstein in time and space: A life in 99 particles.* London: John Murray Press.

Haak, D. C., HilleRisLambers, J., Pitre, E., & Freeman, S. (2011). Increased structure and active learning reduce the achievement gap in introductory biology. *Science, 332,* 1223–1216.

Hackman, M., & Morath, E. (2018). Teachers quit jobs at highest rate on record. Retrieved from https://www.wsj.com/articles/teachers-quit-jobs-at-highest-rate-on-record-11545993052

Hargreaves, A., Ayson, G., & Karunaweera, S. (2024, December). The power of play. Retrieved from https://ascd.org/el/articles/the-power-of-play

Hattie, J. A. C. (2009). *Visible learning: A synthesis of over 800 meta-analyses relating to achievement.* New York: Routledge.

Hattie, J. A. C. (2015, October). We aren't using assessments correctly. *Education Week.* Retrieved from https://www.edweek.org

Holzer, H. (2019). *Monument man: The life & art of Daniel Chester French.* New York: Generic.

Hwang, N. Y., & Kisida, B. (2021). Spread too thin: The effects of teacher specialization on student achievement. *EdWorkingPaper: 21–477.* Annenberg: Brown University. Paper No. 21-477. Retrieved from https://files.eric.ed.gov

Isaacson, W. (2007). *Einstein: His life and universe.* New York: Simon & Schuster.

Ito, T. A., Larsen, J. T., Smith, N. K., & Cacioppo, J. T. (2001, October). Negative information weighs more heavily on the brain: The negativity bias in evaluative categorizations. In Cacioppo, J., Berntson, G., Adolphs, R., Carter, C., Davidson, R., McClintock, M., McEwen, B., Meaney, M. Schacter, D.. Sternberg, E., Suomi, S. & Taylor, S. (Eds.) *Foundations to social neuroscience* (pp. 576–597). Cambridge, MA: MIT Press.

Jensen, E. (2005). *Teaching with the brain in mind.* Alexandria, VA: ASCD.

Jensen, E. (2019). *Poor students, rich teaching: Seven high-impact mindsets for students from poverty.* (Revised ed.). Alexandria, VA: ASCD.

Jensen, E., & McConchie, L. (2020). *Brain-based Learning: Teaching the way students really learn.* (3rd ed.). Thousand Oaks, CA: Corwin.

Joseph, S. (2019, August). Depression, anxiety rising among U.S. college students. Retrieved August 31, 2019 from https://www.reuters.com/article/us-health-mental-undergrads/depression-anxiety-rising-among-us-college-students-idUSKCN1VJ25Z

Jung, C. (1938). *Psychological reflections: A Jung anthology* (Vol. 9). Princeton, NJ: Princeton University Press.

Kallick, B., & Zmuda, A. (2017). *Students at the center: Personalized learning with habits of mind.* Alexandria, VA: ASCD.

Karweit, N., & Slavin, R. E. (1981). Measurement and modeling choices in studies of time and learning. *American Educational Research Journal*, *18*(2), 157–171. https://doi.org/10.2307/1162379.

Kessler, R. (2000). *The soul of education: Helping students find connection, composure, and character at school*. Alexandria, VA: ASCD.

Kincaid, A. (2022, February). The evidence is mounting: Teacher specialization in elementary grades hurts student learning. *National Council on Teacher Quality*. Retrieved June, 2024 from NCTQ.org

Kirschner, P. A., Sweller, J., & Clark, R. E. (2006). Why minimal guidance during instruction does not work: An analysis of the failure of constructivist, discovery, and problem-based, experiential, and inquiry-based teaching. *Educational Psychologist*, *41*, 75–86.

Kohn, A. (2015). *Schooling beyond measure and other unorthodox essays about education*. Portsmouth, NH: Heinemann.

Krajcik, J. S., & Czerniak, C. M. (2013). *Teaching science in elementary and middle school*. (4th ed.). New York: Routledge.

Krajcik, J. S., & Shin, N. (2014). Project-based learning. Retrieved from https://www.researchgate.net

Krathwohl, D. R., Bloom, B. S., & Masia, B. B. (1964). *Taxonomy of educational objectives: Handbook II: Affective domain*. New York: David McKay Company.

Kurtz, H., Lloyd, S. C., & Solis, V. (2024, March). Introducing the teacher moral index. *Education Week*. https://www.edweek.org

Lederman, J. (2024). Massachusetts puts its education excellence at risk. *Wall Street Journal*. Retrieved December 27, 2024 from https://wsj.com

Lepper, M. R., Corpus, J. H., & Iyengar, S. S. (2005). Intrinsic and extrinsic motivational orientations in the classroom: Age differences and academic correlates. *Journal of Educational Psychology*, *97*(2), 184–196.

Lewis, H. (1990). *A question of values: Six ways we make the personal choices that shape our lives*. San Francisco, CA: Harper-Collins.

Lickona, T. (1991). *Educating for character: How our schools can teach respect and responsibility*. New York: Bantam Books.

Locklear, M. (2025, March).. Why don't we remember being a baby? New study provides clues. *Science & Technology*. https://news.yale.edu

Lopes, M. P., & Cunha, M. P. (2008). Who is more positive, the optimist or the pessimist? Exploring the role of hope as a moderator. *Journal of Positive Psychology, 3*(2), 100–109.

Marzano, R. J. (2004). *Building background knowledge for academic achievement.* Alexandria, VA: ASCD.

Marzano, R. J. (2009). Helping students process information. *Educational Leadership, 67*(2), 86–87.

Marzano, R. J., Pickering, D. J., & Pollock, J. E. (2001). *Classroom instruction that works: Research-based strategies for increasing student achievement.* Alexandria, VA: ASCD.

McKibben, S. (2018, October). Grit and the greater good: A conversation with Angela Duckworth. *Educational Leadership, 76*(2), 40–45.

McTighe, J., Self, E., & Wiggins, G. (2004). You can teach for meaning. *Educational Leadership, 62*(1), 26–30.

McTighe, J., & Willis, J. (2019). *Upgrade your teaching: Understanding by design meets neuroscience.* Alexandria, VA: ASCD.

Meacham, J. (2006). *American gospel: God, the founding fathers, and the making of a nation.* New York: Random House.

Mol, S. E., & Bus, A. G. (2011). To read or not to read: A meta-analysis of print exposure from infancy to early adulthood. *Psychological Bulletin, 137*(2), 267.

Newport, C. (2019). *Digital minimalism: Choosing a focused life in a noisy world.* New York: Portfolio.

Odileke, O. (2024, July). How to kill student curiosity in 5 steps (and what to do instead). *Education Week.* Retrieved from https://www.edweek.org

Orlich, D. C., Harder, R. J., Callahan, R. C., Trevisan, M. S., & Brown, A. H. (2007). *Teaching strategies: A guide to better instruction.* (8th ed.). Boston, MA: Houghton Mifflin.

Ormrod, J. E. (2012). *Human learning.* (6th ed.). Upper Saddle River, NJ: Pearson Education, Inc.

Ormrod, J. E. (2019). *Human learning.* (8th ed.). Upper Saddle River, NJ: Pearson Education, Inc.

Ostroff, W. L. (2016). *Cultivating curiosity in K-12 classrooms: How to promote and sustain deep learning.* Alexandria, VA: ASCD.

Payne, A. C., Whitehurst, G. J., & Angell, A. L. (1994). The role of home literacy environment in the development of language ability in preschool children from low-income families. *Early Childhood Research Quarterly, 9*(3–4), 427–440.

Peterson, S. J., & Byron, K. (2008). Exploring the role of hope in job performance: Results from four studies. *Journal of Organizational Behavior, 29*(6), 785–803.

Petrilli, M. J. (2015). The new ESEA will be "loose-loose" because Arne Duncan went overboard with "tight-tight" [blog post]. *Flypaper*. Retrieved from https://edexcellence.net/articles/thenew-esea-will-be-%E2%80%-9Cloose-loose%E2%80%9D-because-arne-duncan-went-overboard-with-5E2%80%9Ctight-tight%E2%80%9D

Phi Delta Kappa Poll of the Public's Attitudes Toward the Public Schools (2019). 51st annual. Retrieved from https://pdkpoll.org

Piaget, J. (1926). *The language and thought of the child*. New York: Harcourt, Brace, & Company.

Piaget, J. (1969). *Psychologie et pedagogie*. Paris: Denoel/Garnier.

Posey, A. (2019). *Engage the brain: How to design for learning that taps into the power of emotion*. Alexandria, VA: ASCD.

Postman, N., & Weingartner, C. (1969). *Teaching as a subversive activity*. New York: Dell.

Price, D. A. (2024, September). 'Supremacy' Review: A competition for tech's future. *The Wall Street Journal*. Retrieved from https://www.wsj.com

Randazzo, S., Barnum, M., & Jargon, J. (2025, January). Screens have taken over classrooms. Even students have had enough. *The Wall Street Journal*. Retrieved from https://www.wsj.com

Rebora, A. (2019, May). Honoring the teen brain: A conversation with Thomas Armstrong. *Educational Leadership, 78*(8), 24–27.

Reeves, D. (2021). *Fearless schools: Building trust and resilience for learning, teaching, and leading*. New York: Creative Leadership Press.

Richardson, D. (2008). Don't dump the didactic lecture; fix it. *Advances in Physiology Education, 32*, 23–24.

Rogers, C. (1969). *Freedom to learn: A view of what education might become*. Columbus, OH: Merrill.

Rosebrough, T. R. (2003). Debunk these 10 myths about teaching and learning. *The Teaching Professor*. New York: Magna Publications.

Rosebrough, T. R., & Leverett, R. G. (2011). *Transformational teaching in the information age: Making why and how we teach relevant to students.* Alexandria, VA: ASCD.

Rosenthal, T. L., & Zimmerman, B. J. (1978). *Social learning and cognition.* New York: Academic Press.

Roth, M. S. (2024). *The student: A short history.* New Haven, CT: Yale University Press.

Rud, A. G., & Garrison, J. (2012). Introduction. In A. G. Rud & J. Garrison (Eds.), *Teaching with reverence: Reviving an ancient virtue for today's schools* (pp. 1–16). New York: Palgrave Macmillan.

Sawyer, R. K. (2006). *The Cambridge handbook of learning sciences.* New York: Cambridge University Press.

Schmoker, M. (2018). *Focus: Elevating the essentials to radically improve student learning.* (2nd ed.). Alexandria, VA: ASCD.

Schultz, B. (2025, January). This school will have AI teach kids (with some human help). Retrieved from https://www.edweek.org

Schultz, W. (2000). *Multiple reward signals in the brain.* National Review Neuroscience.

Schunk, D. H. (2008). *Learning theories: An educational perspective.* (5th ed.). Upper Saddle River, NJ: Pearson.

Schwartz, M., Sadler, P. M., Sonnert, G., & Tai, R. (2008). Depth versus breadth: How content coverage in high school science courses relates to later success in college science coursework. *Science Education, 93*(5), pp. 798–826.

Shaara, M. (1975). *Killer angels: A novel of the civil war.* New York: Ballentine Books.

Sharp, S. D. (2024, June). What schools can learn from a global assessment on creative thinking. *Education Week.* https://www.edweek.org.

Silver, H. F., Strong, R. W., & Perini, M. J. (2007). *The strategic teacher: Selecting the right research- based strategy for every lesson.* Alexandria, VA: ASCD.

Slavich, G. M. (2005, October). Transformational teaching: E-xcellence in teaching (Vol. 5). Retrieved from https://www.georgeslavich.com

Slavich, G. M., & Zimbardo, P. G. (2012). Transformational teaching: Theoretical underpinnings, basic principles, and core methods. *Educational Psychology Review, 24,* 569–608.

Snyder, C. R. (1995). Conceptualizing, measuring, and nurturing hope. *Journal of Counseling & Development, 73*, 355–360.

Snyder, C. R., Rand, K. L., & Sigmon, D. R. (2002). Hope theory: A member of the positive psychology family. In C. R. Snyder & S. J. Lopez (Eds.), *Handbook of positive psychology* (pp. 257–276). New York: Oxford University Press.

St. Jude research highlights (2024, Summer). *St. Jude Inspire, 6*(5), 24–25.

Strasser, D. (2019). Creating classrooms that teach the whole kid. *MiddleWeb*. https://www.middleweb.com.

Svinivki, M., & McKeachie, W. J. (2011). *McKeachie's teaching tips: Strategies, research, and theory for college and university teachers.* (13th ed.). Belmont, CA: Wadsworth.

Takabori, A. (2020, July). How the adolescent brain learns. *The Science of Learning Blog.* Retrieved from https://www.scilearn.com/how-the-adolescent-brain-learns/

Tomasello, M. (2019). *Becoming human: A theory of ontogeny.* Cambridge, MA: Harvard University Press

Tomlinson, C. A. (2000, August). Differentiation of instruction in the elementary grades. *ERIC Digest.* ERIC Clearinghouse on Elementary and Early Childhood Education.

Tuovinnen, J. E., & Sweller, J. (1999). A comparison of cognitive load associated with discovery learning and worked examples. *Journal of Educational Psychology, 91*, 334–341.

Twenge, J. M. (2009). Generational changes and their impact in the classroom: Teaching Generation Me. *Medical Education, 43*, 398–405.

Vygotsky, L. S. (1978). *Mind in society: The development of higher mental process.* Cambridge, MA: Harvard University Press.

Webb, N. (1997). *Research monograph number 6: Criteria for alignment of expectations and assessments on mathematics and science education.* Washington, DC: CCSSO.

Webb, N., Christopherson, S., & Morelan, B. (2023, March). An inside look at Webb's Depth of Knowledge. Retrieved from https://www.edutopia.org

Wenger, E. (1998). *Communities of practice.* Cambridge, MA: Cambridge University Press.

Whitman, R. (2019). Three things our middle school students need most. *MiddleWeb.* https://middleweb.com

Wigfield, A., Eccles, J. S., Schiefele, U., Roeser, R. W., & Davis-Kean, P. (2006). Development of achievement motivation. In N. Eisenberg, W. Damon, & R. M. Lerner (Eds.), *Handbook of child psychology: Social, emotional, and personality development.* (6th ed., pp. 933–1002). John Wiley & Sons, Inc.

Willard, D. (1998). *The divine conspiracy: Rediscovering our hidden life in God.* San Francisco, CA: HarperCollins.

Willis, J. (2024). Guiding students to harness mistakes for learning. Brain-based learning-Edutopia.org. Retrieved from middleweb@smartbrief.com

Wise, M., & Pandolpho, B. (2019, September). Avoiding the siren calls. *Educational Leadership, 77* (1), 22–29.

Wolfe, P. (2010). *Brain matters: Translating research into classroom practice.* (2nd ed.). Alexandria, VA: ASCD.

Yoshinobu, L. (1989). Construct validation of the Hope Scale: Agency and pathways components. Unpublished master's thesis. University of Kansas.

Zacharia, F. (2006). We all have a lot to learn. *Newsweek, 147*(2), 37.

For Product Safety Concerns and Information please contact our EU
representative GPSR@taylorandfrancis.com
Taylor & Francis Verlag GmbH, Kaufingerstraße 24, 80331 München, Germany

www.ingramcontent.com/pod-product-compliance
Lightning Source LLC
Chambersburg PA
CBHW070259230426
43664CB00014B/2579